P9-DHM-909

Modern Critical Interpretations

William Makepeace Thackeray's Vanity Fair

Modern Critical Interpretations

These and other titles in preparation

Modern Critical Interpretations

William Makepeace Thackeray's
Vanity Fair

Edited and with an introduction by

Harold Bloom
Sterling Professor of the Humanities
Yale University

Chelsea House Publishers ◊ *1987*

NEW YORK ◊ NEW HAVEN ◊ PHILADELPHIA

053734

© 1987 by Chelsea House Publishers,
a division of Chelsea House Educational Communications, Inc.,
   95 Madison Avenue, New York, NY 10016
   345 Whitney Avenue, New Haven, CT 06511
   5014 West Chester Pike, Edgemont, PA 19028

Introduction © 1987 by Harold Bloom

Printed and bound in the United States of America

10 9 8 7 6 5 4 3 2 1

∞ The paper used in this publication meets the minimum
requirements of the American National Standard for
Permanence of Paper for Printed Library Materials,
Z39.48–1984.

Library of Congress Cataloging-in-Publication Data
William Makepeace Thackeray's Vanity fair.
   (Modern critical interpretations)
   Bibliography: p.
   Includes index.
   Contents: On Vanity fair / Dorothy van Ghent—Art
and nature / Barbara Hardy—The reader in the
realistic novel / Wolfgang Iser—[etc.]
   1. Thackeray, William Makepeace, 1811–1863.
Vanity fair. [1. Thackeray, William Makepeace, 1811–1863.
Vanity fair. 2. English literature—History and
criticism] I. Bloom, Harold. II. Series.
PR5618.W57 1987   823'.8   87-8019
ISBN 0-87754-747-5 (alk. paper)

Contents

Editor's Note

This book gathers together a representative selection of the best modern criticism devoted to William Makepeace Thackeray's major novel, *Vanity Fair*. The critical essays are reprinted here in the chronological order of their original publication. I am grateful to Wendell Piez for his aid in researching this volume.

My introduction considers the deep affinity between the novel's two strongest characters, Becky Sharp and Thackeray the narrator. Dorothy Van Ghent begins the chronological sequence with her ambivalent appreciation of Becky Sharp, who is seen as representing simultaneously the aggressive exuberance and the destructiveness of our morally confused civilization.

In a meditation upon art and nature in *Vanity Fair*, Barbara Hardy suggests that social criticism is the central aim of the novel. Wolfgang Iser, working in the very different mode of assaying the reader's share in esthetic effect, analyzes Thackeray's manipulations of the reader's habitual expectations.

Visionary satire, a highly oxymoronic genre, is judged by Robert E. Lougy to be exemplified by *Vanity Fair,* which thus takes its place in the center of a tradition with Blake, Wordsworth, and Shelley as forerunners, and Morris, Hardy, and D. H. Lawrence as later sages. The charades in *Vanity Fair* are interpreted in all their "incriminating potential" by Maria DiBattista, who finds in them another series of instances of Thackeray's pervasive "moral and ideological ambivalence."

Robert M. Polhemus, reading *Vanity Fair* as comedy, uncovers in its style the shifting perspectives of defiance and fatalism, both of which Thackeray needs and instructs us to need. In this volume's final essay, H. M. Daleski unveils the strategies of *Vanity Fair* in order to argue that the novel, "despite its inconsistent narrator and seemingly divided worlds, is all of a piece."

Introduction

G. K. Chesterton, saluting Thackeray as the master of "allusive irrelevancy," charmingly admitted that "Thackeray worked entirely by diffuseness." No celebrator of form in the novel has ever cared for Thackeray, who, like his precursor Fielding, always took his own time in his writing. Thackeray particularly follows Fielding, who was the sanest of novelists, in judging his own characters as a magistrate might judge them, a magistrate who was also a parodist, and a vigilant exposer of social pretensions. Charlotte Brontë, Thackeray's fierce admirer, in her preface to the second edition of *Jane Eyre,* said that he "resembles Fielding as an eagle does a vulture." This unfortunate remark sounds odd now, when no critic would place Thackeray anywhere near Fielding in aesthetic eminence. Nor would any critic wish to regard Thackeray as Dickens's nearest contemporary rival, a once fashionable comparison. Thackeray, we all agree, is genial but flawed, and until recently he did not have much following among either novelists or critics. Trollope and Ruskin sometimes seem, respectively, the last vital novelist and great critic to regard Thackeray with the utmost seriousness. Splendid as he is, Thackeray is now much dimmed.

Though *Henry Esmond* is a rhetorical triumph in the genre of the historical novel, *Vanity Fair,* itself partly historical, is clearly Thackeray's most memorable achievement. Rereading it, one encounters again two superb characters, Becky Sharp and William Makepeace Thackeray. One regrets that Becky, because of the confusion of realms that would be involved, could not exercise her charms upon the complaisant Thackeray, who amiably described his heroine's later career as resembling the slitherings of a mermaid. Anyway, Thackeray probably shared the regret, and what I like best in *Vanity Fair* is how much Thackeray likes Becky. Any reader who does not like Becky is almost certainly not very likeable herself or himself. Such an observation may not seem like literary criticism to a formalist or some other kind of plumber, but I would insist that Becky's vitalism is the critical center in any strong reading of *Vanity Fair*.

Becky, of course, is famously a bad woman, selfish and endlessly designing, and rarely bothered by a concern for truth, morals, or the good of the community. But Thackeray, without extenuating his principal personage, situates her in a fictive cosmos where nearly all the significant characters are egomaniacs, and none of them is as interesting and attractive as the energetic Becky. Her will to live has a desperate gusto which is answered by the gusto of the doubtless fictive Thackeray who is the narrator and who shares many of the weaknesses that he zestfully portrays in his women and men. Perhaps we do not so much like Becky because Thackeray likes her, as we like Becky because we like that supreme fiction, Thackeray the narrator. Sometimes I wish that he would stop teasing me, and always I wish that his moralizings were in a class with those of the sublime George Eliot (she would not have agreed, as she joined Trollope and Charlotte Brontë in admiring Thackeray exorbitantly). But never, in *Vanity Fair,* do I wish Thackeray the story-teller to clear out of the novel. If you are going to tour Vanity Fair, then your best guide is its showman, who parodies it yet always acknowledges that he himself is one of its prime representatives.

Does Thackeray overstate the conventional case against Becky, in the knowing and deliberate way in which Fielding overstated the case against Tom Jones? This was the contention of A. E. Dyson in his study of irony, *The Crazy Fabric* (1965). Dyson followed the late Gordon Ray, most genial and Thackerayan of Thackerayans, in emphasizing how devious a work *Vanity Fair* is, as befits a narrator who chose to go on living in Vanity Fair, however uneasily. Unlike Fielding, Thackeray sometimes yields to mere bitterness, but he knew, as Fielding did, that the bitter are never great, and Becky refuses to become bitter. An excessively moral reader might observe that Becky's obsessive lying is the cost of her transcending of bitterness, but the cost will not seem too high to the imaginative reader, who deserves Becky and who is not as happy with her foil, the good but drab Amelia. Becky is hardly as witty as Sir John Falstaff, but then whatever other fictive personage is? As Falstaff seems, in one aspect, to be the child of the Wife of Bath, so Becky comes closer to being

Falstaff's daughter than any other female character in British fiction. Aside from lacking all of the Seven Deadly Virtues, Becky evidently carries living on her wits to extremes in whoredom and murder, but without losing our sympathy and our continued pleasure in her company.

I part from Dyson when he suggests that Becky is Vanity Fair's Volpone, fit scourge for its pretensions and its heartlessness, of which she shares only the latter. Becky, like her not-so-secret sharer, Thackeray the narrator, I judge to be too good for Vanity Fair, though neither of them has the undivided inclination to escape so vile a scene, as we might wish them to do. Becky's most famous reflection is: "I think I could be a good woman if I had five thousand a year." This would go admirably as the refrain of one of those ballads that Brecht kept lifting from Kipling, and helps us to see that Becky Sharp fits better into Brecht's world than into Ben Jonson's. What is most winning about her is that she is never morose. Her high-spirited courage does us good and calls into question the aesthetics of our morality. Thackeray never allows us to believe that we live anywhere except Vanity Fair, and we can begin to see that the disreputable Brecht and the reputable Thackeray die one another's lives, live one another's deaths, to borrow a formulation that W. B. Yeats was too fond of repeating.

Thackeray, a genial humorist, persuades the reader that *Vanity Fair* is a comic novel, when truly it is as dark as Brecht's *The Threepenny Opera* or his *Rise and Fall of the City of Mahagonny.* The abyss beckons in nearly every chapter of *Vanity Fair,* and a fair number of the characters vanish into it before the book is completed. Becky survives, being indomitable, but both she and Thackeray the narrator seem rather battered as the novel wanes into its eloquent and terribly sad farewell:

> Ah! *Vanitas Vanitatum!* Which of us is happy in this world? Which of us has his desire? or, having it, is satisfied?— Come children, let us shut up the box and the puppets, for our play is played out.

On *Vanity Fair*

Dorothy Van Ghent

Almost exactly a century separates *Tom Jones* from *Vanity Fair;* but with *Vanity Fair,* so far as technical developments in the novel are concerned, it is as if there had been none. We are in the storytelling convention of the "omniscient author" sanctioned by Fielding's great example, but with a damaging difference that is due, not so much to an inherent inadequacy of that convention itself, as the spiritual incoherency of another age. It is true that the technique of omniscient authorship can allow a relaxed garrulity—what James called "the terrible fluidity of self-revelation"—for if the author can enter the story in his own voice, there is nothing to keep him from talking. After discussing Becky's adolescent designs on Jos Sedley, and her visions of shawls and necklaces and aristocratic company which she imagines will be the rewards of marriage with Jos, Thackeray comments, "Charming Alnaschar visions! it is the happy privilege of youth to construct you, and many a fanciful young creature besides Rebecca Sharp has indulged in these delightful day-dreams ere now!" The comment is both inane and distracting—distracting our attention from the tense mental operations of Becky and turning it upon the momentarily flaccid mentality of her author. The effect is one of rather surprised irritation, as it is again when, having described Jos's wardrobe, his pains in dressing, his vanity and shyness, Thackeray remarks, "If Miss Rebecca can get the better of *him,* and at her first entrance into life, she is a young person of no ordinary cleverness."

From *The English Novel: Form and Function.* © 1953 by Dorothy Van Ghent. Harper & Brothers, 1961

What we feel is that two orders of reality are clumsily getting in each other's way: the order of imaginative reality, where Becky lives, and the order of historical reality, where William Makepeace Thackeray lives. The fault becomes more striking in the following unforgivable parenthesis. Jos has just presented Amelia with flowers. " 'Thank you, dear Joseph,' said Amelia, quite ready to kiss her brother, if he were so minded. (And I think for a kiss from such a dear creature as Amelia, I would purchase all Mr. Lee's conservatories out of hand.)" The picture of Thackeray himself kissing Amelia pulls Amelia quite out of the created world of *Vanity Fair* and drops her into some shapeless limbo of Thackerayan sentiment where she loses all aesthetic orientation.

Nevertheless, the conventions employed in a work of art cannot fairly be judged by themselves; they can be judged only as instrumental to a vision. The time in which Thackeray wrote was, compared with Fielding's time, itself looser in what we might call cultural composition; its values were less integrated in a common philosophical "style" or tenor of mind. In *Tom Jones,* the convention of the author's appearance in his book as "gregarious eye," stage manager, and moralist, is a strategy that is used with a highly formal regularity of rhythm, and it animates every turn of Fielding's language, as the ironic life of the language. Most important, the convention had benefited by an age's practice of and belief in form, form in manners and rhetoric and politics and philosophy—that is, by an age's coherently structured world view. The set of feelings and ideas of which Fielding acts as vehicle, when he makes his personal appearances in his book, is a set of feelings and ideas with the stamp of spiritual consistency upon them. They do not afflict us with a sense of confused perspectives between the author's person and his work, his opinions and his creation, as do Thackeray's. Whereas Thackeray seems merely to be victimized or tricked by his adopted convention into a clumsy mishandling of perspectives, Fielding manipulates the same convention deliberately to produce displacements of perspective as an organic element of composition. This is not to say that Fielding's creative perceptions are, on the whole, more penetrating and profound than Thackeray's; indeed, Thackeray's seem to reach a good deal deeper into the difficulties, compromises, and darkness of the human estate; but Fielding's have the organizing power to make an ancient oral convention of storytelling an appropriate instrument of his vision, whereas the same convention—actually one that is most

sympathetic to Thackeray's gift of easy, perspicacious, ranging talk—
becomes a personal convenience for relaxation of aesthetic control,
even a means to counterfeit his creative vision.

Becky ruminates, "I think I could be a good woman if I had five
thousand a year," and adds with a sigh, "Heigho! I wish I could
exchange my position in society, and all my relations, for a snug sum
in the Three per Cent. Consols." Here she is as true to herself psy-
chologically as is Moll Flanders; but she is more complex than Moll,
and we know perfectly that, at this promising stage of her career, the
sigh is only a casual fantasy—arising chiefly out of boredom with the
tedious business of cultivating the good graces of people much less
intelligent than herself—and that if the "snug sum" were offered, she
would not really exchange her prospects for it, for her temperament
is not at present to be satisfied with snugness. There are to be pearl
necklaces, presentation at court, *a succès fou* at Gaunt House. But
Thackeray interprets for us: "It may, perhaps, have struck her that to
have been honest and humble, to have done her duty, and to have
marched straightforward on her way, would have brought her as
near happiness as that path by which she was striving to attain it."
This is a doctrine with which, in principle, we have no cause either
to agree or disagree; a novel is not made of doctrines and principles,
but of concretely imagined life, and whatever moral principle may be
honestly adduced from that life must be intrinsic to it, concretely
qualitative within it. *Vanity Fair* is strong with life, but in those
concretions where it is alive there is nothing to suggest that to be
"honest and humble" can possibly bring happiness. Becky is the
happiest person in the book; she is alive from beginning to end, alive
in intelligence and activity and *joie de vivre,* whether she is throwing
Dr. Johnson's dictionary out of a coach window, in superb scorn of
the humiliations of the poor, or exercising her adulterous charm on
General Tufto, whether she is prancing to court to be made an "honest woman" (in stolen lace), or hiding a cognac bottle in a sordid bed.
From Becky's delighted exercise in being alive, we can learn nothing
about the happiness to be derived from humble dutifulness. On the
other hand, from Amelia's humble dutifulness we can learn nothing
that convinces us doctrinally that happiness lies in such a way of life.
For it is not only that the brisk gait and vivid allure of Becky's
egoistic and aggressive way of life make Amelia look tepid, tear
sodden, and compromised: this effect would not occur if the book
were soundly structured, if its compositional center (what James

called the "commanding centre" of the composition) were entirely firm and clear.

The actually functioning compositional center of *Vanity Fair* is that node or intersection of extensive social and spiritual relationships constituted by Becky's activities: her relationships with a multitude of individuals—Jos and Amelia and George, old Sir Pitt and Rawdon and Miss Crawley and the Bute Crawleys and the Pitt Crawleys, Lady Bareacres, Lord Steyne, and so on—and, through these individuals, her relationships with large and significant blocks of a civilization: with the middle-class Sedley block, that block which is in the process of physical destruction because of its lack of shrewdness in an acquisitive culture; with the other middle-class Osborne block, that block which has displaced the Sedley block through its own acquisitive shrewdness and through the necessarily accompanying denial of the compassionate and sympathetic human impulses; with the aristocratic Crawley block, in all its complexity of impotence and mad self-destruction, and (in young Sir Pitt, with the "gooseberry eyes") canny self-renovation through connivance with the economy and morality of the dominant middle class; with the ambiguous Steyne block, that is above the economic strife and therefore free of conventional moral concerns, but in its social freedom, "stained" deeply in nerves and blood. (In the names he gives people, Thackeray plays—like many novelists—on punning suggestion, as he does in the name of the crawling Crawleys, "raw-done" Rawdon, Sharp, Steyne, O'Dowd, etc.) This social relationship, concretized through Becky's relationship with individuals, is the hub of the book's meanings, its "compositional center." But beside this violently whirling and excited center is another, a weak and unavailing epicenter, where Amelia weeps and suffers and wins—wins Dobbin and solvency and neighborhood prestige and a good middle-class house with varnished staircases. Organized around the two centers are two plots, which have as little essentially to do with each other as Thackeray's creative imagination had to do with his sentimental, morally fearful reflections. He cannot bear to allow the wonderfully animated vision of Becky's world to speak for itself, for its meaning is too frightening; he must add to it a complementary world—Amelia's—to act as its judge and corrector. One thinks, in comparison, of Balzac, who was writing almost contemporaneously. Balzac was both as skeptical and as sentimental as Thackeray, but he was a passionate rationalist as well, and a much bolder dramatic formalist.

In Balzac, the weak and the suffering and the pure in heart do not win. They have no pretensions to effective moral dynamism in the evil Balzacian world, which uses them as illustrative examples of the impotence of an "honest and humble" way of life.

As the convention of the omniscient author allows Thackeray to keep up a maladroit "sound track" of personal interpolations, so it also collaborates with his confusion as to where the compositional center of his book lies; for though the Becky-world and the Amelia-world, having no common motivation, confront each other with closed entrances, so to speak, yet the author is able, by abuse of his rights of omniscience, to move facilely through these closed doors. We assume that, in Thackeray's plan, the compositional center of the book was to be the moral valence between the two worlds. But there is no valence between them, nothing in either to produce a positive effect of significance on the other. The only effect is negative: the Amelia-plot pales into a morally immature fantasy beside the vivid life of the Becky-plot. For Becky is the great morally meaningful figure, the moral symbol, in the book, and beside her there is room and meaning for Amelia only as victim—certainly not as "success figure." The word "moral" . . . needs perhaps a somewhat closer attention here. Becky is not virtuous, and in speaking of her as a morally significant figure, we cannot possibly confuse her moral meaning with the meaning of "virtue." She is a morally meaningful figure because she symbolizes the morality of her world at its greatest intensity and magnitude. The greediness that has only a reduced, personal meaning in Mrs. Bute Crawley, as she nags and blunders at old Miss Crawley's deathbed, acquires, through Becky's far more intelligent and courageous greed—as she encounters international techniques for the satisfaction of greed with her own subtle and knowing and superior techniques—an extensive social meaning. The corruption that, in old Sir Pitt, has meaning at most for the senility of a caste, becomes, in Becky's prostitution and treason and mur-derousness, the moral meaning of a culture. For Becky's activities are designed with intelligent discrimination and live intuition, and they are carried through not only with unflagging will power but with joy as well. By representing her world at its highest energetic potential, by alchemizing all its evil but stupid and confused or formless im-pulses into brilliantly controlled intention, she endows her world with meaning. The meaning is such as to inspire horror; but the very fact that we conceive this horror intellectually and objectively is an acknowledgment of Becky's morally symbolic stature.

There is a French criticism of the English novel, that, in the English novel's characteristic concern with the social scene, it fails to explore "the deeper layers of personality." One understands the motivation of this criticism, if one compares representative French and English novels of approximately the same periods, although the criticism itself does not seem to be well thought out. *The Pilgrim's Progress* is populated with social "types," sparsely limned sketches that isolate certain traits, whereas, almost contemporaneously, Madame de Lafayette's *La Princesse de Clèves* is concentrated upon a depth illumination of the tortured psyche of a delicate woman who, in a loveless marriage, is moved by an illicit passion. Even *Clarissa Harlowe,* which is commonly thought of as an exhaustive representation of a young woman's emotions, is, because of its mythical qualities, rather more of a vision into the social soul than into that of a credible individual; and the difference is brought out by comparison with the almost contemporaneous *Manon Lescaut,* by the Abbé Prévost, in which the subject has certain affinities with that of *Clarissa* (except that it is the girl, here, who is the libertine, and the young man who is the afflicted one), but which is again—like so many French novels—a concentrated depth drawing of personal psychology rather than a social vision. One could pursue a number of other examples in the same way. But the difference is a relative difference only. For the "deeper layers of personality" are meaningless unless they can be related, at least by inference, to aspects of life that have some social generality; while social life is meaningless unless it finds embodiment in individuals. A more significant difference between classical French novels and classical English novels is one of method. The English novel has tended traditionally to symbolize certain phases of personality through the concrete image (Christian as the "man in rags" with a burden on his back; the Philosopher Square standing among Molly's "other female utensils" when the curtain falls in the bedroom; Clarissa, with streaming eyes and disheveled bosom, prostrating herself before Lovelace; Jaggers washing his hands or Miss Havisham beside the rotten bridecake); while the French novel has tended traditionally to a discursive analysis of feeling and motive, as has the French drama. Image and analysis are merely two different ways of mirroring what goes on in the soul. The methods are never exclusive; and we find such significant exceptions to the general tendency as Flaubert's *Madame Bovary,* where the image dominates, and Conrad's *Lord Jim,* where analysis dominates.

Let us illustrate, from *Vanity Fair,* the method of the image and what it is able to imply as to the "deeper layers of personality." Characteristically, in this book, the social concern is paramount. We have spoken of the various "blocks" of this civilization, some slipping into rubble by the crush of the others or by internal decay, some thrusting themselves up by the neighboring defaultment. But governing all the movements is one ethos of aggressive egoism, articulated through the acquisition of cash and through the prestige fantasies born of cash. Becky herself is a member of no particular class and confined to no particular "block." (Significantly, she is the daughter of a Bohemian artist and a French music-hall singer.) She is more mobile than any of the other characters, because of her freedom from caste, and thus is able to enter into a great variety of class relationships: this is the peculiar novelistic virtue of the picara and picaro, and the enduring source of virility of the picaresque form—the protagonist's freedom of movement. Still acting under the same ethos as that governing the whole civilization, Becky is able to represent its tendencies without class pretenses. Thus Becky, like Moll Flanders, though a strongly individualized character, is the type of a whole civilization, a small-scale model of a world, a microcosm in which the social macrocosm is subtilized and intensified and made significant. With this predominantly social bearing of the novel, the characters—even Becky—tend to be depicted in a relatively "external" way: that is, there is relatively little discussion of the nuances of their feelings and their motivations; they are not self-analytical characters, as characters in French novels tend to be, nor do they spend much time in deliberate analysis of each other; they appear to us physically, in action; and—with some generalized interpretive help from the author himself (whose interpretations, as we have noted, we cannot always trust)—we enter into their motives and states of feeling by our own intuition. Examples are manifold. There is Becky's meeting of George's eyes in the mirror as she and Amelia, Jos and George, are leaving for Vauxhall: a flashing, accidental illumination of his vanity and vulnerability—and though here might be an excellent opportunity for Becky to engage in psychological speculations and deliberations, little of the kind occurs. There is the physical flash, the illumination by image only, and Becky has George's number. And yet later, when George and Amelia, Becky and Rawdon, meet on their honeymoon trips at Brighton, and Becky with almost unconscious slyness encourages George to make love to her, the early image of the meeting of eyes in a mirror plays on the reader's understanding of motivation, as it does again when we see Becky in overt sexual aggressiveness at the Brussels ball. There has been no need of discursive analysis of motive; the image does the work.

Or—another instance of the work of the image—there is Jos, in his obesity and his neckcloths and his gorgeous waistcoats. We should not expect Jos to analyze himself, nor anyone else to have an interest in analyzing what he feels, for he is below the level of what is rationally interesting; and yet, from the physical picture alone, we are made intuitively aware of deeply disturbed "layers of personality" in Jos. He is one of the most complicated psychological portraits in the book (more complicated, for instance, than that of another voluptuary, the Marquis of Steyne, who has more refined opportunities than Jos and a better head), extremely unpleasant, with suggestions of impalpable submerged perversities, pathetic, with a pathos that is at the same time an outrage to our feeling for what is humanly cognizable in pathos—for Jos is a glandularly suffering animal, with the "human" so hidden in his tortured fat that we feel it to be obscene, while we must still recognize it as human. Jos offering his neck to Isidore's razor (in the passage we have quoted in the general introduction to the present volume) is a complex image of a kind of fear so muddied, an image of a psychological state so profoundly irrational, that we react to it with an impulse of horrified laughter— the intuitive horror having no other outlet than in a sense of the absurd. At the same time that these physical images of Jos flash to the mind's eye an impression of something deep and possible in individual personality, they are made by Thackeray to represent to the social reason an extremely significant phase of a culture. We see in Jos's obesity the sickness of a culture, the sickness due to spiritual gourmandism, or, in simpler but still metaphorical words, to "overeating"; in his shyness of women, the repressions and abnormalities of a sick culture; in his stupidity and febrile conceit, the intellectual numbing and tubercular euphoria of a culture. Thus the physical image, here, mirrors most fearful depths of the personal and, at the same time, most threatening perspectives of the social life.

We shall cite a few more illustrations of this method of the "image," as Thackeray uses it, keeping in mind its double significance, its significance for personal psychology (the "deeper layers of personality") and its social significance. But in preparation for these particular citations, we should speak of one singularly important theme of *Vanity Fair*, and that is a theme which we shall call the theme of the "fathers." In the eighteenth-century novels that we have read, the "father" has appeared in a light that is rather different from the light that is thrown on the "father" in nineteenth-century novels. There is Squire Allworthy, for instance, who, as "father," though he may have his failures of insight, is still an affirmative moral reference in the *Tom Jones* system of values; he is idealized, but this itself is significant of the fact that the "father" still represents a moral ideal. In the eighteenth century, the idea of the "father" was not, on the whole, ambiguous, or suggestive of doubts or deficiencies or culpability—that is, as this idea is reflected in literature. Mr. Harlowe, in *Clarissa,* is the most exceptional example; but even here, the daughter's return to her "Father's house," on the elevated stage of the divine, is an affirmation and sanction of the usual parental-filial relationship of authority and obedience which is esteemed to be universally valid; Mr. Harlowe made a mistake, but so did Clarissa make a mistake; informed by Clarissa's passion, it is to be hoped that no other daughters or fathers will ever make such mistakes. In *Tristram Shandy,* the "father," Walter Shandy, is a freak, yet he is presented only under the aspect of general human freakishness, pleasant and interesting eccentricity, and we are led in no way to think of him in terms of parental culpability; indeed, as "father," he takes his responsibility most enormously—to be the right kind of father and to bring up the right kind of son are his devouring concern; the inquiries and devotions of fatherhood—as to conditions of conception, size of the son's nose, the son's name, his education—form the whole shape of Walter Shandy's mental activities, his very eccentricity. Similarly in Smollett's *Humphry Clinker,* where the "father" (an uncle, in this case) is a querulous hypochondriac, leading his life in a tone of objection to everything, we are "on his side," we object when he objects, with a grain of salt for his elderly fury; and the book has its moral equipoise in the rightness of this "father's" perceptions.

We see, in the notion of the father in eighteenth-century literature, a reflection of social trust: of trust in and reliance upon and devotion to a general social system of values—that coherent "world view" of the eighteenth century that we have spoken of earlier in this essay. For, under our anciently inherited patriarchal organization of the family, an organization that inevitably extended itself into political organization and philosophic organization, the "father-imago" has acquired vast symbolic extension beyond domestic life and into general social life: our "fathers" are not only our individual fathers but all those who have come before us—society as it has determined our conditions of existence and the problems we have to confront. *Vanity Fair,* with its panorama of western European international society as backdrop to the heroine's activities, is full of "fathers," sick fathers, guilty fathers.

Curiously enough, we have seen the inception of the theme of the "fathers" in Jane Austen, despite her eighteenth-century social sensibility; and it is—along with her inception of modern technique in the handling of the "point of view"—a striking mark of her modernity. In *Pride and Prejudice,* the father, Mr. Bennet, is anything but the morally idealized figure of Squire Allworthy; and even as an "eccentric" or "humorous" character (in the older sense), he casts moral shadows that, for instance, Walter Shandy—another "eccentric"—does not cast. Mr. Bennet, as father, is guilty. In Dickens's *Great Expectations,* we have seen that the theme of the "father" dominates the meanings of the book, and we have seen how many inflections Dickens is able to get out of this theme. Crossing language boundaries, we find in Stendhal's *The Red and the Black* (1830) various implementations of the same theme: Julien's revolt against the peasant grossness of his own father, and his finding of a "spiritual father" in a Jansenist monk, who himself is under suspicion from the religious institution to which he belongs (here the father who is worthy of respect is himself virtually a social outcast). In Balzac's *Père Goriot*—whose title is indicative of the "father" theme—the actual father, Goriot, is a degenerative victim of corrupt social ideas, while the "spiritual father" of the hero is an out-and-out criminal. Turgenev's *Fathers and Sons* announces the same theme by its title; and again here the "fathers" are inadequate. In Dostoyevski's *The Brothers Karamazov,* the sons' murder of the father is the focus of plot, and we have the famous question, on the part of Ivan Karamazov, "Who doesn't desire his father's death?" The title of D. H. Lawrence's *Sons and Lovers* indicates again the modern preoccupation with the parental-filial relationship. Joyce's *Portrait of the Artist* and his *Ulysses* carry out the same preoccupation: in the former, the hero's actual father goes to pieces and the family disintegrates with him; in the latter, the hero's "spiritual father" is a Jew, emotionally an alien in the Dublin of the book, without integration with the social body, and as lost and wandering as the son.

It is significant of the vital intuitiveness of Thackeray's *Vanity*

Fair that the theme of the "fathers" should have such importance: in this book, an immensely impressive female, herself quite fatherless, manages to articulate in her career the most meaningful social aspects of the "father" theme. We need, in this view of the book, to free ourselves from the narrower Freudian aspects of the theme and to think in terms of Thackeray's broad social perspective, where the "fathers" are such variants as Mr. Sedley, Mr. Osborne, old Sir Pitt, even the Marquis of Steyne: in other words, such variants as to include all the older, authoritative, and determinative aspects of society.

And now, with this general notion of the significance of the theme of parental authority, we can consider that Thackeray manages to get out of the "image" of old Mr. Osborne and his daughters coming down the stairs, in their evening ritual, to dinner.

> The obedient bell in the lower regions began ringing the announcement of the meal. The tolling over, the head of the family thrust his hands into the great tail-pockets of his great blue coat and brass buttons, and without waiting for a further announcement, strode downstairs alone, scowling over his shoulder at the four females.
>
> "What's the matter now, my dear?" asked one of the other, as they rose and tripped gingerly behind the sire.
>
> "I suppose the funds are falling," whispered Miss Wirt; and so, trembling and in silence, this hushed female company followed their dark leader.

In the lines just before this there is one other, inconspicuous, touch: in the drawing room where they are waiting for dinner is a chronometer "surmounted by a cheerful brass group of the sacrifice of Iphigenia." The depths which are suggested by this picture, but quite as if accidentally, are the depths of Greek tragedy and, still further back, of Freud's dim, subhuman, imagined "primitive horde": the "dark leader" with his "hushed female company," and the ridiculous but furious Victorian clock "cheerfully" symbolizing the whole. Antiquity's dark brooding over the monstrous nature of man is made to take on, in this incidental image of a family's going to dinner, the unwholesomeness and perversity that have been added to man's classical monstrosity by "falling funds," a drop in the stock market.

There is the recurrent incident in the hall outside the bedroom where old Miss Crawley is sick, Becky tending her, everyone—

including Becky—waiting for and speculating on the "reversionary spoils."

> Captain Rawdon got an extension of leave on his aunt's ill-
> ness, and remained dutifully at home. He was always in her
> ante-chamber. (She lay sick in the state bedroom into which
> you entered by the little blue saloon.) His father was always
> meeting him there; or if he came down the corridor ever so
> quietly, his father's door was sure to open, and the hyaena
> face of the old gentleman to glare out. What was it set one
> to watch the other so? A generous rivalry, no doubt, as to
> which should be most attentive to the dear sufferer in the
> state bedroom. Rebecca used to come out and comfort both
> of them—or one or the other of them rather.

Short and unemphasized as the passage is (outside of the ironic line, it consists only of an image, the image of Rawdon opening a door and looking into the corridor, of the old man's "hyaena face" in-stantly looking out from an opposite door, of Becky coming down the hall to "comfort" them), it contains a pregnant and disturbing meaning, both for personal psychology and for social psychology. Later, when Becky will attempt to inform Sir Pitt about her clan-destine marriage, but without telling him the name of her husband, he will be uproariously amused; but as soon as she tells him the name—his son, Rawdon—he goes mad with inexplicable fury. We look back mentally to the incidents in the hall outside Miss Crawley's sickroom, where son and father glare at each other, and where Becky comes to comfort them *separately,* holding each in suspense as to her amorous favor. And we look forward also to that horrible line in Becky's letter to Rawdon (after the disclosure of Sir Pitt), where she says, "I might have been somebody's mamma, instead of—Oh, I tremble, I tremble . . ." What it contained here is probably the most excruciatingly primitive father-son battle in literature, with one of the most sensitively feminine but perversely sentimental reflections upon it. How are we to say, in such a case, whether what we are observing is the "deeper layers of personality" or the social scene?

And then there is the description of the turmoil surrounding old Sir Pitt's death. It consists of a succession of images: Miss Horrocks flitting in ribbons through "the halls of their fathers"; again Miss Horrocks "of the guilty ribbons, with a wild air, trying at the presses and escritoires with a bunch of keys"—while upstairs they are "trying to bleed" Sir Pitt (the "trying to" suggests unknown but repulsive derangements); the servant girl screaming and making faces at him in private while he whimpers. The cumulation of these images, scattered and casual as they are, makes the face of a gorgon of destiny. The personal and social idea of the "father" (an idea which is inextricably both personal and social) is made the nasty companion of the ribbon-flitting Miss Horrocks; when Sir Pitt gives the family pearls to Lady Jane ("Pretty pearls—never gave 'em to the ironmonger's daughter"), marital relationships, with all they mean for the security created for us by our elders, are referred back retrospectively to Sir Pitt's chronic tipsiness and Lady Crawley's worsted knitting—an "enormous interminable piece of knitting"—"She worked that worsted day and night. . . . She had not character enough to take to drinking"; drawers are tried while the "father" is bled; and finally—so great is the prestige of this "father" and baronet—the servant girl has full amplitude to scream obscenities and make faces at him, for he has turned into "a whimpering old idiot put in and out of bed and cleaned and fed like a baby."

The burden of Thackeray's intuition into personal psychology and its social meaning falls on images like these, and they are innumerable in *Vanity Fair*. But the greatness of *Vanity Fair* is not in scattered images, sensitive as these are. They are all gathered up in Becky Sharp. Becky does for Jos, murderously, at the end; and what she does to Jos is only cancerously implicit in himself and the civilization that has made him; she is the darkness—shining obsidianly in an intelligent personality—in old Mr. Osborne's dense sadism against his daughters and his corruption of the meaning of paternal responsibility toward his son; she manipulates the insane father-son conflict between Sir Pitt and Rawdon; and she is the "guilty ribbons" of Miss Horrocks (instead of a servant's ribbons she has a courtesan's pearls) and at the same time the whimpering idiocy of the dying Sir Pitt (paralleling his repulsive attack of mortality, she inflicts a similarly repulsive mortality on Jos)—for she is at once all the imperatively aggressive, insanely euphoric impulses of a morally sick civilization and an individual condensation of that civilization. We question whether we would understand her at all, or be charmed by her buoyancy or appalled by her destructiveness, if her impulses were not memorabilia of our own and her civilization our heritage.

Art and Nature

Barbara Hardy

> Thence passing forth, they shortly do arriue,
>   Whereas the Bowre of Blisse was situate;
>   A place pickt out by choice of best aliue,
>   That natures worke by art can imitate:
>   In which what euer in this worldly state
>   Is sweet, and pleasing vnto liuing sense,
>   Or that may dayntiest fantasie aggrate,
>   Was poured forth with plentifull dispence,
> And made there to abound with lauish affluence.
>
> Goodly it was enclosed round about,
>   Aswell their entred guestes to keepe within,
>   As those vnruly beasts to hold without;
>   Yet was the fence thereof but weake and thin;
>   Nought feard their force, that fortilage to win,
>   But wisedomes powre, and temperaunces might,
>   By which the mightiest things efforced bin:
>   And eke the gate was wrought of substaunce light,
> Rather for pleasure, then for battery or fight.
>   The Faerie Queene, bk. 2, can. 12

One of the major implications of the title and main image of *Vanity Fair* is the corruption of nature by greed, deceit and art. Thackeray approves of honesty, sincerity and spontaneity, and criticizes posing and artifice. The critical emphasis varies, falling on heartlessness or hypocrisy or exhibitionism or artful manipulation, and sometimes on all four simultaneously. Everyone knows that the chief perfor-

From *The Exposure of Luxury: Radical Themes in Thackeray*. © 1972 by Barbara Hardy. Peter Owen Ltd., 1972.

mance in *Vanity Fair* is that given by "the famous little Becky puppet," as Thackeray describes her in the preliminary address, "Before the Curtain." At the very beginning of her performance, in chapter 1, "Chiswick Mall," Thackeray does not show Becky's accomplishments as artist, actress and performer, but rather establishes the environment in which performance becomes necessary. He begins his novel with a critique of Becky's environment which certainly goes far to create and explain her histrionic ways: it shows a hierarchy of power, a pecking-order in which Becky is as yet only finding her way, and it very clearly reveals the incompatibility of success—defined as money and power—with nature, heart, sincerity or love. As yet, Becky is only a novice and learner, as befits a character who is on the brink of leaving school. Her performance has scarcely begun, but Thackeray's analysis of performance is already complex.

The school itself is one of those totally assimilated social symbols which exist in full and self-contained particularity in Thackeray's satiric world: schooling, learning, achievement, testimonials, teaching, finishing the course, are metaphors as well as realities, but Thackeray uses the ready-made social symbol very quietly. It is his great gift, here and elsewhere, to work through a plenitude of such unobtrusively significant action, and not only each detail of pedagogy, teaching and learning, but every single aspect of the scene, events and characters, in this first chapter, is morally expressive.

One key to the theme of art and nature is given in the first image, which contrasts the undignified with the dignified. It does so in a way which draws our attention to the narrow formality of the institution which Becky and Amelia are about to leave for the wide world. The fat horses and the fat coachman, the bandy-legged servant and the red nose of Miss Jemima Pinkerton represent the vivid, undignified informal world, while "the great iron gate of Miss Pinkerton's academy for young ladies" represents dignity and enclosure. The contrast becomes plainer in the first piece of dialogue between Miss Pinkerton and her sister Miss Jemima, who are a contrasting pair in a novel largely organized on the principle of contrast and duality. The contrast emerges as one of style and sensibility, directing our attention to Miss Jemima's natural, informal, good-hearted, outer-directed attention and the formality and arrangement of Miss Pinkerton's artifice:

"It is Mrs Sedley's coach, sister," said Miss Jemima. "Sambo, the black servant, has just rung the bell; and the coachman has a new red waistcoat."

"Have you completed all the necessary preparations incident to Miss Sedley's departure, Miss Jemima?" asked Miss Pinkerton herself.

(Chap. 1)

Miss Jemima speaks loosely, but has her eye on the colours and particulars of the world outside. Her concreteness is indeed characteristic of Thackeray's descriptions, and throughout the novel his eye is fixed on the solidity and detail of persons, clothing and objects; his presentation of Amelia and Becky, for instance, is marked by this precision, of action and colour. Here, the concreteness makes Miss Jemima interesting, while her sister is less attractive in her dryness and abstraction of style. The Johnsonian lady, Miss Pinkerton, speaks in the grand style; she is presented appropriately by Thackeray in polysyllabic, allusive and high-piled grandeur, as he sets the linguistic tone for the ensuing dialogue: "Miss Pinkerton herself, that majestic lady; the Semiramis of Hammersmith, the friend of Dr Johnson, the correspondent of Mrs Chapone herself." His grand style acts as a faint burlesque, not pushing its effects, but maintaining grandeur of vocabulary and syntax. The contrast between the sisters becomes explicit when Miss Jemima uses the old word "bowpot" and is told to say "bouquet" as more genteel, doing her best in the compromise of "booky," which is followed up by the big-hearted but undignified simile, "as big almost as a haystack." The sisters' styles draw attention to the formality and pedantry of the one and the clumsy and casual artlessness of the other; and throughout Thackeray works in circumlocutions, like "autograph letter" or "billet," and in typically Johnsonian figures of sentiments and negation, parallelism and more periodic elaboration, all shown paradigmatically in this model letter:

MADAM,—After her six years' residence at the Mall, I have the honour and happiness of presenting Miss Amelia Sedley to her parents, as a young lady not unworthy to occupy a fitting position in their polished and refined circle. Those virtues which characterise the young English gentlewoman, those accomplishments which become her birth and station, will not be found wanting in the amiable Miss Sedley, whose *industry* and *obedience* have endeared her to her instructors, and whose delightful sweetness of temper has charmed her *aged* and her *youthful* companions.

In music, in dancing, in orthography, in every variety of embroidery and needle-work, she will be found to have realised her friends' *fondest wishes.* In geography there is still much to be desired; and a careful and undeviating use of the backboard, for four hours daily during the next three years, is recommended as necessary to the acquire-ment of that dignified *deportment* and *carriage,* so requisite for every young lady of *fashion.*

(Chap. 1)

What is said is as important as how it is said, but style and value are related. Miss Pinkerton's careful and pedantic "For whom is this, Miss Jemima?" is answered by the artless and warm-hearted "For Becky Sharp: she's going too," which undermines the style and the very insistence of Miss Pinkerton's question. Thackeray works through dialogue and through the surrounding narration and de-scription. The humanity of Miss Jemima's unpedantic, unpremedi-tated natural style matches her spontaneous show of sensibility: she trembles, blushes all over "her withered face and neck," and her sensibility shows itself in her wasted imaginative identification with Becky, "it's only two and ninepence and poor Becky will be miser-able if she don't get one." Miss Jemima, like Briggs later on, is much too simple-minded to criticize the grand and acquisitive cold-heartedness around her, but her criticism is implicit in the language and feelings. Predatory Miss Pinkerton is coldly, self-interestedly and manipulatively in control, in giving, speaking, teaching and writing; Miss Jemima is vulgar, loving, giving, artlessly betrayed by feeling and undignified in action and speech, trotting off, ungrandly, "exceedingly flurried and nervous." Miss Pinkerton's condolence is a public event: "Once, when poor Miss Birch died of the scarlet fever, was Miss Pinkerton known to write personally to the parents of her pupils; and it was Jemima's opinion that if anything *could* console Mrs Birch for her daughter's loss, it would be that pious and eloquent composition in which Miss Pinkerton announced the event."

From the beginning, therefore, Thackeray establishes a contrast between formal showing-off and lack of heart, loving generosity and lack of style. He also establishes, from the beginning, a sense of social hierarchy and power-structure, not unrelated to the style and capacity for feeling. Those who are at the top, in Vanity Fair, get there by art, not heart. The linguistic and moral contrast between the "superior" and the "inferior" sister is followed by the contrast between two other ladies in the hierarchy, Becky and Amelia: "Miss Sedley's papa was a merchant in London, and a man of some wealth; whereas Miss Sharp was an articled pupil, for whom Miss Pinkerton had done, as she thought, quite enough, without conferring upon her at parting the high honour of the Dixonary." The psychological pecking order can override the social, as Thackeray demonstrates in the little passage in which Becky makes her "adieux" in fluent French, unintelligible to Miss Pinkerton, thus inflicting a stylistic victory, appropriately enough, over the Johnsonian mode. This victory is accompanied by a flouting gesture, as Becky refuses to accept one of Miss Pinkerton's fingers: "In fact, it was a little battle between the young lady and the old one, and the latter was worsted." One could describe the whole action of the novel in such military terms, and Thackeray uses them freely; he is well aware of ironic parallels between his story and history, and also of the "unheroic" appropriation of military or heroic terms to everyday strife. In his novels, these skirmishes are fought with social weapons—with words, sentences, wit, foreign languages, gestures, rituals, refusal of ritual, clothes, presents. Thackeray does more than show Becky as victorious, her strength of personality, intelligence and learning prevailing over her low place in the social order. He creates a contrast between failure and success in artifice and ritual. Miss Pinkerton makes her ridiculous, elaborate gesture, "she waved one hand, both by way of adieu, and to give Miss Sharp an opportunity of shaking one of the fingers of the hand which was left out for that purpose," and Becky nonchalantly rejects it. Becky's very last gesture, however, is not an act of social aggression against the style of the Hammersmith Semiramis, but a rejection of poor loving styleless Jemima. The throwing of the dictionary is of course a marvellous rejection of style—Johnson, the institution, order, dignity and pretence—but it is not a simple revolutionary gesture which we can applaud. As so often, Becky is on the wrong side, attacking the establishment only because she is jealous of its advantages. Our sympathies are carefully withdrawn from her as she throws back what is not only a symbol of "corrupt" style, but a loving present. Miss Jemima's very last speech and action are typically artless, broken and stammered, and her last generous, if silly, act, is accompanied by the words, "God bless you!" Becky, like Scrooge, rejects a blessing. The rejection marks her entry into the great world.

Thackeray's last sentences emphasize the contrast between the world of school and the great world, as the gates close; he says, formally, "and so, farewell to Chiswick Mall." The brilliant close-up of this first scene has established style and theme, the style and theme of nature and art.

There are certain characters in this chapter I have not mentioned, and they too are involved in style and theme. They are the author and his readers, real and imaginary. Before the curtain rises, in "Before the Curtain," Thackeray has presented himself as the Manager of the Performance; he has begun to develop the histrionic significance, as well as the vanity and commerce of Vanity Fair; he has admitted that he is in it for money, and is not without charlatanry: amongst the crowd he singles out "quacks (*other* quacks, plague take them!)" The author is, from the beginning, involved in the business of art and acting. As we know, Thackeray originally intended to call the novel "A Novel without a Hero" and to develop the theme of unheroic drama, rather than that of Vanity Fair. Although there are divergent emphases, the two themes very plainly overlap, and in Thackeray's claim to the unheroic, he uses the convention of the self-conscious artist to make a certain claim for realism. A certain claim: implicit in his insistence that this is art, that these are puppets, that this is illusion and performance, that it is a book, written for money by an author, and read by various readers, is the claim that it is closer to life and nature than some forms of art. The self-conscious claim to realism is made in the description of Amelia's undignified, unheroinelike beauty and sensibility. Another complex claim for heart as against art, it ends with a disarming address to a Reader, Jones, whose taste is "for the great and heroic in life and novels" and who will underline the author's "foolish, twaddling, etc.," and add *"quite true."* But Jones is critically presented as a worldling, reading at his club, and "rather flushed with his joint of mutton and half-pint of wine," and it seems likely that Thackeray uses him in order to further the claim for simple, unworldly heroines and passions. He does as much as he can to claim that his novel, though a work of art, has a heart, and not simply by making jokes about the wrong kind of heartless, art-seeking (but wine-flushed) reader like Jones, but by deliberately drawing attention to his own sentimentality. Amelia has a heart, cries over silly novels and dead pets, and attracts heart: in yet another qualification of the pecking order, even Semiramis gives orders that Amelia should be treated gently, and when Amelia goes she is surrounded by loving, giving, weeping friends. Indeed, Becky is not entirely the victim of the class hierarchy, since Amelia's friends are seen to love her for herself ("kindly, smiling, tender, gentle, generous heart") and perhaps even Miss Pinkerton is not sensitive to her wholly because of her father's income. Though Becky is made to claim, in chapter 2, "In Which Miss Sharp and Miss Sedley Prepare to Open the Campaign," that Amelia was her only friend, we shall, in retrospect, blame that on Becky's heartlessness rather than on the social hierarchy of the school. Jones's rejection of Amelia is made to be a rejection of sentimentality, and Thackeray lays claim to the sentimental as an index of sensibility: she cries over dead pets, lost friends and even silly novels. Thackeray makes it awkward for us by linking the three so that we cannot be as selective in our emotional snobbishness as we should like.

Amelia is, as a character and a woman, deliberately sentimental: that is, she is meant to be the sentimental heroine of an unsentimental novel, illustrating the complexity of the heart's excesses. We shall begin by loving her and feeling with her, in her friendship, love, grief, maternal affection, but we shall eventually learn the limitations of sensibility uncontrolled by reason: she will worship her unworthy husband, alive and dead, spoil her son, and make sentimental demands on Dobbin, her patient lover. The very first chapter prepares us for this aspect of Thackeray's criticism, his refusal to accept unqualified sensibility as a moral norm. Heart like this can be linked with silliness and excess: it is all very well to cry for dead birds but not for silly novels. But the qualification of heart is less conspicuous, at first, than the qualification of art. Only in the misplaced loving gift of Miss Jemima, the rejected dictionary, do we see our first clear instance of sentimentality; it is punished rudely by its exact opposite, hard-heartedness, which also earns its first clear criticism when, biting the hand that feeds, it throws back the dictionary at the silly affectionate old woman. The reader is involved even with her rejection, because Thackeray tells us, drily, that she is not going to appear again:

> Miss Jemima had already whimpered several times at the idea of Amelia's departure; and, but for fear of her sister, would have gone off in downright hysterics, like the heiress (who paid double) of St Kitt's. Such luxury of grief, however, is only allowed to parlour-boarders. Honest Jemima had all the bills, and the washing, and the mending, and the puddings, and the plate and crockery, and the servants to superintend. By why speak about her? It is probable that we shall not hear of her again from this moment to the end of time, and that when the great filigree iron gates are once closed on her, she and her awful sister will never issue therefrom into this little world of history.
>
> (Chap. 1)

What does this rather odd passage mean? That there are heroines even less heroic than Amelia, who is, once this passage has urged us to reflect, more of a heroine than Miss Jemima? Thackeray seems to mean what he says in the sentence "Such luxury of grief, however, is only allowed to parlour-boarders." In a novel which is about the luxury of grief, Thackeray reminds us, in the dismissal of Jemima, of the circumstances that permit grief, in and out of novels. He also claims for his novel a high degree of realism; though it is interesting to distinguish his claim from George Eliot's in the totally tolerant *Adam Bede,* where Lizbeth Bede *is* permitted her "luxury of grief." At the same time, he draws our attention to the social interest of his emotional theme: if people like Amelia dwell on grief, devote themselves to worship of dead husband and living son, it is as a luxury. Thus he makes another qualification of heart: sensitivity, as well as art, depends on position and possessions. Thackeray's initial creation of category is uncomfortably blurred. On the one hand we have Miss Pinkerton, the Johnsonian style, the great filigree iron gates, Jones, with his contempt for sentiment, and Becky, able to put down the grand style with fluent French. On the other hand, Amelia, all tolerant and sentimental readers, and Jemima, loving, giving, artless. Between the two worlds, the rejection of the dictionary; yet, beside it, Jemima's blessing and the two-edged admission that Jemima is not promising material for Thackeray's novel.

The realistic effects of the self-conscious reference should be stressed here. Thackeray insists on the illusion, the art, the performance, the drama, the novel, but in such a way—dismissing a character who is not qualified to be a character—that brings the novel very close indeed to life. There are some unpromising materials, he says, that will not come in; and the very mention reminds us of the novelist's selection from life, in a way that is moving and evaluative. At the extreme of art is Thackeray himself; at the extreme of heart is Jemima, who will be left out. The reader is made wary, and perhaps, as Thackeray wished, uncomfortable. If he is attentive, he will not reject Jones, Amelia, Miss Pinkerton or Johnson's dictionary too precipitately. This first formal and framing scene in chapter 1 of *Vanity Fair* makes plain the heroines' initiation into the great world, and the reader's initiation into the world of the novel. In chapter 8, Thackeray draws our attention, first by direct dramatic presentation, then by complex authorial commentary, to certain crucial differences between Becky's art and his own. In the chapters that bridge the initiation and the very explicit analysis, we have seen Becky beginning her career as an artist in life. She does, in fact, possess some positive artistic talents, chiefly displayed in her entertaining and persuasive performances of miming and singing. In chapter 8, Thackeray adds a new artistic achievement, epistolary and literary. Becky's letter to Amelia probably takes a glance at epistolary fiction in its feminine effusiveness and self-pity, and its very lack of resemblance to the situations of Pamela and Clarissa. But the chief purpose, as I see it, is to bridge Becky's artistic forte, which is dramatic, and Thackeray's, which is literary.

Becky is given the whole narrative burden, for the space of her letter, of introducing the reader to a new place and several new characters. She is a quite convenient surrogate for Thackeray, being, like him, sharply attentive, witty and satirical, but she is of course not simply a surrogate, and her letter also shows the Becky Sharp traits of false sensibility and predatoriness. Her letters are usually written to get something, directly or indirectly, and this letter is clearly designed to keep a tenuous hook on the Sedleys—"Is your poor brother recovered of his rack-punch?"—and even Amelia, who may be good for another India muslin or pink silk in the future. But the cast-off dresses are still fresh (see chapter 11 for the hint about their replacements) and Thackeray is free to develop Becky's literary gifts.

Throughout the novel, her letters are important in the furthering of the action and the development of her character. There is the unsuccessful letter dictated to Rawdon and addressed to Miss Crawley, which does not take in the old lady for a minute, since Becky has thought of using short sentences but not of misspelling. Moreover, the letter is fatally amusing, and Miss Crawley detects Becky's fundamental style, as well as appreciating it and asking for more. There is the more crucial letter written to Rawdon in the sponging-house, designed to put him off affectionately and humorously, but unable to hide her exhibitionism and self-interest. Its crude ingratiation does not take in Rawdon, who also detects her fundamental style, failing to be amused by Becky's jokes, and disliking them for the first time. But the first letter, in chapter 8, is a more disengaged venture. It introduces the reader to King's Crawley and to some new and important characters. It is a superb stroke of art, totally and variously eloquent. The very title of the chapter, "Private and Confidential," is expressive of the epistolary gossip of bosom-friends and its frank-mark, "Free.-Pitt Crawley," is informative and ironic—who pays and for what, or who does not pay, is always of interest in Thackeray.

MY DEAREST, SWEETEST AMELIA,

With what mingled joy and sorrow do I take up the pen to write to my dearest friend! Oh, what a change between to-day and yesterday! *Now* I am friendless and alone; yesterday I was at home, in the sweet company of a sister, whom I shall ever, *ever* cherish!

I will not tell you in what tears and sadness I passed the fatal night in which I separated from you. *You* went on Tuesday to joy and happiness, with your mother and *your devoted young soldier* by your side; and I thought of you all night, dancing at Perkins's, the prettiest, I am sure, of all the young ladies at the Ball. I was brought by the groom in the old carriage to Sir Pitt Crawley's town house, where, after John the groom had behaved most rudely and insolently to me (alas! 'twas safe to insult poverty and misfortune!), I was given over to Sir P's care, and made to pass the night in an old gloomy bed, and by the side of a horrid gloomy old charwoman, who keeps the house. I did not sleep one single wink the whole night.

Sir Pitt is not what we silly girls, when we used to read Cecilia at Chiswick, imagined a baronet must have been.

Anything, indeed, less like Lord Orville cannot be imagined. Fancy an old, stumpy, short, vulgar, and very dirty man, in old clothes and shabby old gaiters, who smokes a horrid pipe, and cooks his own horrid supper in a saucepan. He speaks with a country accent, and swore a great deal at the old charwoman, at the hackney coachman who drove us to the inn where the coach went from, and on which I made the journey *outside for the greater part of the way*. . . .

"There's an avenue," said Sir Pitt, "a mile long. There's six thousand pounds of timber in them there trees. Do you call that nothing?" He pronounced avenue—*eveneu*, and nothing—*nothink*, so droll. . . .

Here, my dear, I was interrupted last night by a dreadful thumping at my door; and who do you think it was? Sir Pitt Crawley in his night-cap and dressing gown, such a figure! As I shrank away from such a visitor, he came forward and seized my candle; "no candles after eleven o'clock, Miss Becky," said he. "Go to bed in the dark, you pretty little hussey (that is what he called me), and unless you wish me to come for the candle every night, mind and be in bed at eleven." And with this, he and Mr Horrocks the butler went off laughing. You may be sure I shall not encourage any more of their visits. They let loose two immense blood-hounds at night, which all last night were yelling and howling at the moon. . . .

Half an hour after our arrival, the great dinner-bell was rung, and I came down with my two pupils (they are very thin and insignificant little chits of ten and eight years old). I came down in your *dear* muslin gown (about which that odious Mrs Pinner was so rude, because you gave it me); for I am to be treated as one of the family, except on company days, when the young ladies and I are to dine up-stairs.

Well, the great dinner-bell rang, and we all assembled in the little drawing-room where my Lady Crawley sits. She is the second Lady Crawley, and mother of the young ladies. She was an ironmonger's daughter, and her marriage was thought a great match. She looks as if she had been handsome once, and her eyes are always weeping for the loss of her beauty. She is pale and meagre, and high-shouldered; and has not a word to say for herself, evidently. Her step-son, Mr Crawley, was likewise in the room. He was in full dress, as pompous as an undertaker. He is pale, thin, ugly, silent; he has thin legs, no chest, hay-coloured whiskers, and straw-coloured hair. He is the very picture of his sainted mother over the mantel-piece—Griselda of the noble house of Binkie. . . .

Lady Crawley is always knitting the worsted. Sit Pitt is always tipsy, every night; and, I believe, sits with Horrocks, the butler. Mr Crawley always reads sermons in the evenings; and in the morning is locked up in his study, or else rides to Mudbury, on county business, or to Squashmore, where he preaches, on Wednesdays and Fridays, to the tenants there.

A hundred thousand grateful loves to your dear papa and mamma! Is your poor brother recovered of his rack-punch? Oh, dear! Oh, dear! How men should beware of wicked punch!

Ever and ever thine own,

REBECCA

The first thing we notice is the conventional satire on female sensibility. The strongest impression is that of exaggeration and falsity: "My Dearest, Sweetest Amelia"; or "With what mingled joy and sorrow do I take up the pen to write to my dearest friend! . . . Now I am friendless and alone." But these initial emotions of indulgence, envy and self-pity soon give way to the sheer verve of narrative and presentation of character. Thackeray does something simple but clever with Becky's narration; he allows it to overlap slightly with his own narrative in chapter 10, so that we see a slight discrepancy between what has happened and what Becky presents as happening. Nothing very marked; just a little evidence that Becky is a liar: the detail that she has not slept a wink (when the author has said that she does) and the omission of her attempt to pump the old charwoman with whom she shares a bed. She presents herself as the heroine of a Gothic novel rather than a resilient, unfastidious and predatory opportunist. But what is most striking is the wit and humour of Becky's narrative, achieved at the expense of the characters in her story. The girls are "very thin and insignificant little chits of ten and eight years old." Lady Crawley "looks as if she had been handsome once, and her eyes are always weeping for the loss of her beauty." Pitt Crawley is "pompous as an undertaker . . . pale, thin, ugly, silent; he has thin legs, no chest, hay-coloured whiskers, and straw-coloured hair." Sir Pitt is exposed by his "dumpy little legs" and rustic accent. The butler is laughed at for his ludicrous French pronunciation (Becky's pride in her French is one of her humourless weaknesses), and Miss Horrocks, described as "very much over-dressed," flings Becky a look of scorn as "she plumped down on her knees."

Such strokes of wit and ridicule may be enjoyed for their own sake, and our critical spirit may be held in check until Thackeray himself stands back to analyse the letter. The contrast between the maidenly gush and the hard-hitting satire is probably clear, but we do not feel strongly critical until Thackeray drily observes that we should. For although he has been using Becky as a narrator, the narration is itself material for satire. It is satire proffered for the reader's enjoyment, then analysed by the satirist.

> Everything considered, I think it is quite as well for our dear Amelia Sedley, in Russell Square, that Miss Sharp and she are parted. Rebecca is a droll funny creature, to be sure; and those descriptions of the poor lady weeping for the loss of her beauty, and the gentleman "with hay-coloured whiskers and straw-coloured hair," are very smart, doubt-less, and show a great knowledge of the world. That she might, when on her knees, have been thinking of some-thing better than Miss Horrocks's ribbons, has possibly struck both of us. But my kind reader will please to re-member, that this history has "Vanity Fair" for a title, and that Vanity Fair is a very vain, wicked, foolish place, full of all sorts of humbugs and falsenesses and pretensions. And while the moralist, who is holding forth on the cover (an accurate portrait of your humble servant), professes to wear neither gown nor bands, but only the very same long-eared livery in which his congregation is arrayed: yet, look you, one is bound to speak the truth as far as one knows it, whether one mounts a cap and bells or a shovel-hat; and a deal of disagreeable matter must come out in the course of such an undertaking.
>
> (Chap. 8)

This first ironic combination of criticism and defence is Thackeray at his most subtle and disconcerting: we cannot know what he is saying in this first paragraph which neatly balances indictment with justification, and relates Becky to her author. But what does he mean by speaking the truth? Does he refer to his own exposure of Becky? Or does he also include her exposure of the vanity and foolishness of Lady Crawley, Pitt and Miss Horrocks, who are all easily and accurately describable as vain and foolish, "full of all sorts of humbugs and falsenesses and pretensions."

Another contrast and symmetrical figure follow: the story of a preacher—a Neapolitan story-teller—who worked himself up into such a "rage and passion" against "some of the villains whose wicked deeds he was describing and inventing that the audience could not resist it." The result of the story-teller's fervour was a good profit: "the hat went round, and the bajocchi tumbled into it, in the midst of a perfect storm of sympathy." This anecdote is balanced against that of the Parisian actors who refuse to play villains and prefer to play virtuous characters for a lower payment. He observes: "I set these two stories one against the other, so that you may see that it is not from mere mercenary motives that the present performer is desirous to show up and trounce his villains; but because he has a sincere hatred of them, which he cannot keep down, and which must find a vent in suitable abuse and bad language." Not a simple antithesis, it needs careful analysis before we finally conclude that Thackeray is admitting his own lack of pure motivation. After all, he is a performer who gains from the performance, an author earning his living with this serial (later a book) which is paid for by the reader. Thackeray is distinguishing between his satiric stance and Becky's; he is telling us clearly that though a critic, she is subjected to the author's criticism as "one who has no reverence except for prosperity, and no eye for anything beyond success. Such people there are living and flourishing in the world—Faithless, Hopeless, Charityless; let us have at them, dear friends, with might and main."

This disclosure criticizes and clarifies Becky's wit and ridicule. While admitting that Thackeray writes for gain, it claims that his satiric mode derives from Faith, Hope and Charity. It invokes lofty and noble moral purpose: he is mercenary but not "merely" mercenary. If we then look at Thackeray's irony, scorn, wit and ridicule, we see that his satire is not cynical; rather it derives from Hope and Faith in the possibilities of human nature, and has Charity. Thackeray is a master of timing and placing, and follows this criticism of Becky's immoral and eclectic satire and wit by a conspicuously charitable and serious satiric piece in the next chapter. Another instance of symmetry and juxtaposition, it is also an instance of Thackeray's explicitness and clarity. Uncomfortable though he may be as a satirist constantly involving the reader in the satire, he takes no chances with misunderstanding. He is writing a novel about the corruption of nature, and this corruption shows itself here, in Becky, performance, wit and satire. However, as an artist sharing the actions of performance, wit and satire, he is constrained to distinguish between right and wrong wit, right and wrong satire. The distinctions involve an art which has a heart—Hope, Faith, Charity—and an art which is heartless, "no reverence for anything except for prosperity." At the same time, he is aware and forced to admit that he is involved in profiting too. The character and the author are fully compared and contrasted. This is extremely rare in English fiction, apart from the earlier and influential case of Fielding who presented, in *Tom Jones,* antithetical images of his own desire for lofty Fame and worldly prosperity—what Thackeray, memorably recalling Fielding's invocation of roast beef, calls "a little of the Sunday side."

Chapter 8, then, exposes Becky as a heartless artist practising Thackeray's arts, and implies that Thackeray is more honourable than Becky. Chapter 9 follows with a demonstration, taking a revised look at those characters analysed so heartlessly and artfully by Becky. Sir Pitt, Lady Crawley and Mr Pitt Crawley are all presented afresh, with wit and satire, and with sympathy and charity. Sir Pitt, for whom admittedly little can be said, is shown as first marrying "under the auspices of his parents," then marrying to please himself. There is feeling in "He had his pretty Rose, and what more need a man require than to please himself?" What follows is inside information, not mere brilliant superficial wit, and it is much more devastating than Becky's exposure: "So he used to get drunk every night: to beat his pretty Rose sometimes: to leave her in Hampshire when he went to London for the parliamentary session, without a single friend in the whole world." An extremely charitable account of pretty Rose herself follows, together with a glance at her limitations and losses: "she had no sort of character, nor talents, nor opinions, nor occupations, nor amusements, nor that vigour of soul and ferocity of temper which often falls to the lot of entirely foolish women. . . . O Vanity Fair—Vanity Fair! This might have been, but for you, a cheery lass:—Peter Butt and Rose, a happy man and wife."

There is a dignified and sympathetic account of Pitt, his respect for his mother-in-law, his kindness, and then—just in case we were beginning to identify Thackeray's manner of satiric analysis with charity and imagination—a devastating account of his mediocrity, industry and lack of self-knowledge. Thackeray's own wit is disarmingly produced when least expected, as we nod over his ability to see the humanity of these characters with heart and generosity; it is harder than anything achieved by Becky's rather visual ridicule: "yet he failed somehow, in spite of a mediocrity which ought to have insured any man a success. He did not even get the prize poem, which all his friends said he was sure of." Thackeray is very deliberate in his revision of Becky's satire, even to the extent of commenting when he agrees with her: "Miss Sharp's accounts of his employment at Queen's Crawley were not caricatures. He subjected the servants there to the devotional exercises before mentioned, in which (and so much the better) he brought his father to join." The parentheses of course mark, once more, the comment Becky would not be capable of making.

Thackeray's expansion and revision has one last effect. He has a capacity for moral and social diagnosis and generalization which Becky, at least at this stage in her education, utterly lacks. She sees, at school and out of it, how she is at an unfair disadvantage because of her birth and poverty; but later, when she makes the celebrated suggestion that she could be a good woman on five thousand a year, she does not see into the heartlessness of Vanity Fair, having insufficient heart and vision for the enterprise. Her social criticism, even when generalized, is shallow. Thackeray, having like Becky observed Sir Pitt's drunkenness and illiteracy, though more seriously and less amusedly, also sees the criticism of society involved in marking the defects of this dignitary. Becky finds Sir Pitt funny; "Anything, indeed, less like Lord Orville cannot be imagined," she comments, in her literary and hypocritically fastidious way. Thackeray replaces this with a moral fervour:

> Vanity Fair—Vanity Fair! Here was a man, who could not spell, and did not care to read—who had the habits and the cunning of a boor: whose aim in life was pettifogging: who never had a taste, or emotion, or enjoyment,

but what was sordid and foul; and yet he had rank, and honours, and power, somehow: and was a dignitary of the land, and a pillar of the state. He was high sheriff, and rode in a golden coach. Great ministers and statesmen courted him; and in Vanity Fair he had a higher place than the most brilliant genius or spotless virtue.

(Chap. 9)

At one stroke, Thackeray candidly admits his own involvement; he makes explicit and dramatic the seriousness, profundity and passion of his satire. Avoiding a simple division of intellect or feeling into art and nature, he creates an art which is as close to nature, and as inclusive and serious, as possible. He also suggests, craftily and dramatically, that social criticism is his aim.

The Reader in the Realistic Novel: Esthetic Effects in Thackeray's *Vanity Fair*

Wolfgang Iser

"You must have your eyes forever on your Reader. That alone constitutes . . . Technique!" Ford Madox Ford's exhortation to the novelist draws attention to one of the few basic rules that have governed the novel throughout its relatively short history. This awareness as a prerequisite for steering the reader has always exerted a fundamental influence on the form of the narrative. From the start the novel as a "genre" was virtually free from traditional constraints and so the novelists of the eighteenth century considered themselves not merely as the creators of their works but also as the law-makers. The events they devise also set out the standards regarded as necessary for judging the events; this is shown clearly by Defoe and Richardson in their prefaces and commentaries, and especially by Fielding in the innumerable essays with which he permeates his narrative. Such interventions are meant to indicate how the author wants his text to be understood, and also to make the reader more deeply aware of those events for the judgment of which his own imagination has to be mobilized. With the author manipulating the reader's attitude, the narrator becomes his own commentator and is not afraid to break into the world he is describing in order to provide his own explanations. That this is a deliberate process is demonstrated by a sentence from Fielding's *Tom Jones:* "And this, as I could not prevail on any of my actors to speak, I myself was obliged to declare."

From *The Implied Reader: Patterns of Communication in Prose Fiction from Bunyan to Beckett.* © 1974 by the Johns Hopkins University Press.

And so the novel as a form in the eighteenth century is shaped by the dialogue that the author wishes to conduct with his reader. This simulated relationship gives the reader the impression that he and the author are partners in discovering the reality of human experience. In this reader-oriented presentation of the world, one can see an historical reflection of the period when the possibility of a priori knowledge was refuted, leaving fiction as the only means of supplying the insight into human nature denied by empirical philosophy.

The author-reader relationship, which was thus developed by the eighteenth-century novel, has remained a constant feature of narrative prose and is still in evidence even when the author seems to have disappeared and the reader is deliberately excluded from comprehension. While Fielding offers this reassurance to his readers: "I am, indeed, set over them for their own good only, and was created for their use, and not they for mine," Joyce, at the other end of the scale drops only the ironic information that the author has withdrawn behind his work, "paring his fingernails." The reader of modern novels is deprived of the assistance which the eighteenth-century writer had given him in a variety of devices ranging from earnest exhortation to satire and irony. Instead, he is expected to strive for himself to unravel the mysteries of a sometimes strikingly obscure composition. This development reflects the transformation of the very idea of literature, which seems to have ceased to be a means of relaxation and even luxury, making demands now on the capacity of understanding because the world presented seems to have no bearing on what the reader is familiar with. This change did not happen suddenly. The stages of transition are clearly discernible in the nineteenth century, and one of them is virtually a half-way point in the development: the so-called "realistic" novel. An outstanding example of this is Thackeray's *Vanity Fair*. Here, the author-reader relationship is as different from the eighteenth-century "dialogue" as it is from the twentieth-century demand that the reader find for himself the key to a many-sided puzzle. In Thackeray, the reader does have to make his own discoveries, but the author provides him with unmistakable clues to guide him in his search.

The first stage in our discussion must be to modify the term "author." We should distinguish, as Wayne Booth does in his *Rhetoric of Fiction*, between the man who writes the book (author), the man whose attitudes shape the book (implied author), and the man who communicates directly with the reader (narrator): "The 'implied author' chooses, consciously or unconsciously, what we read; . . . he is the sum of his own choices. . . . This implied author is always distinct from the 'real man'—whatever we may take him to be—who creates a superior version of himself, a 'second self,' as he creates his work." The narrator, of course, is not always to be identified with the implied author. In the novels of the nineteenth century it happens again and again that the narrator moves even further and further away from the implied author by virtue of being an actual character in the story itself. Traces of this kind of narrator are already apparent in Dickens's novels, and in Thackeray's *Vanity Fair* he is a complete character in his own right. It is almost as if the implied author, who devised the story, has to bow to the narrator, who has a deeper insight into all the situations. What the implied author describes is interpreted by the narrator to a degree far beyond what one might normally deduce from the events. One is bound to ask the purpose of this clear though sometimes complex separation between narration and commentary, especially in a "realistic" novel which is supposed to represent reality as it is. The justification lies in the fact that even a realistic novel cannot encompass total reality. As Arnold Bennett once remarked: "You can't put the whole of a character into a book." If the limitations of the novel are such that one cannot reveal a complete character, it is even more impossible to try to transcribe complete reality. And so even a novel that is called realistic can present no more than particular aspects of a given reality, although the selection must remain implicit in order to cloak the author's ideology.

II

Thackeray's *Vanity Fair* is also governed by this principle, which is clearly reflected by the different titles of the original version and the final one. The first, consisting of eight chapters, was called "Pen and Pencil Sketches of English Society," indicating that the reality described was meant primarily as a reproduction of social situations; the final version, "Vanity Fair," is concerned less with depicting social situations than with offering a judgment of them. This quality is commented on by Thackeray himself in a letter written a few years after the publication of *Vanity Fair:* "the Art of Novels *is* . . . to convey as strongly as possible the sentiment of reality—in a tragedy or a poem or a lofty drama you aim at producing different emotions;

the figures moving, and their words sounding, heroically." "Sentiment of reality" implies that the novel does not represent reality itself, but aims rather at producing an idea of how reality can be experienced. Thus *Vanity Fair* not only offers a panorama of contemporary reality but also reveals the way in which the abundance of details has been organized, so that the reader can participate in the organization of events and thus gain the "sentiment of reality." This is the reason why the novel continues to be effective even today, though the social conditions it describes are only of historical interest. If the past has been kept alive, this is primarily due to the structural pattern through which the events are conveyed to the reader: the effect is gained by the interplay between the implied author who arranges the events, and the narrator who comments on them. The reader can only gain real access to the social reality presented by the implied author, when he follows the adjustments of perspective made by the narrator in viewing the events described. In order to ensure that the reader participates in the way desired, the narrator is set up as a kind of authority between him and the events, conveying the impression that understanding can only be achieved through this medium. In the course of the action, the narrator takes on various guises in order to appear as a fully developed character and in order to control the distance from which the reader has to view the scenes unfolded before him.

At the start of the novel, the narrator introduces himself as "Manager of the Performance," and gives an outline of what the audience is to expect. The ideal visitor to "Vanity Fair" is described as a "man with a reflective turn of mind"; this is an advance indication of what the reader has to accomplish, if he is to realize the meaning of the proceedings. But at the same time, the Manager promises that he has something for everyone: "Some people consider Fairs immoral altogether, and eschew such, with their servants and families: very likely they are right. But persons who think otherwise, and are of a lazy, or a benevolent, or a sarcastic mood, may perhaps like to step in for half an hour, and look at the performances. There are scenes of all sorts: some dreadful combats, some grand and lofty horse-riding, some scenes of high life, and some of very middling indeed; some love-making for the sentimental, and some light comic business." In this way the Manager tries to entice all different types of visitors to enter his Fair—bearing in mind the fact that such a visit will also have its after-effects. When the reader has been following the narrator for quite some time, he is informed: "This, dear friends and companions, is my amiable object—to walk with you through the Fair, to examine the shops and the shows there; and that we should all come home after the flare, and the noise, and the gaiety, and be perfectly miserable in private." But the reader will only feel miserable after walking through the Fair if, unexpectedly, he has come upon himself in some of the situations, thereby having his attention drawn to his own behavior, which has shone out at him from the mirror of possibilities. The narrator is only pretending to help the reader—in reality he is goading him. His reliability is already reduced by the fact that he is continually donning new masks: at one moment he is an observer of the Fair, like the reader; then he is suddenly blessed with extraordinary knowledge, though he can explain ironically that "novelists have the privilege of knowing everything"; and then, toward the end, he announces that the whole story was not his own at all, but that he overheard it in a conversation. At the beginning of the novel the narrator is presented as Manager of the Performance, and at the end he presents himself as the reporter of a story which fell into his hands purely by chance. The further away he stands from the social reality depicted, the clearer is the outline of the part he is meant to play. But the reader can only view the social panorama in the constantly shifting perspectives which are opened up for him by this Protean narrator. Although he cannot help following the views and interpretations of the narrator, it is essential for him to understand the motivations behind this constant changing of viewpoints, because only the discovery of the motivations can lead to the comprehension of what is intended. Thus the narrator regulates the distance between reader and events, and in doing so brings about the esthetic effect of the story. The reader is given only as much information as will keep him oriented and interested, but the narrator deliberately leaves open the inferences that are to be drawn from this information. Consequently, empty spaces are bound to occur, spurring the reader's imagination to detect the assumption which might have motivated the narrator's attitude. In this way, we get involved because we react to the viewpoints advanced by the narrator. If the narrator is an independent character, clearly separated from the inventor of the story, the tale of the social aspirations of the two girls Becky and Amelia takes on a greater degree of objectivity, and indeed one gains the impression that this social reality is not a mere narration but actually exists. The narrator can then be regarded as a sort of mediator between the reader and the events, with the implication that it is only through him that the social reality can be rendered communicable in the first place.

III

The narrator's strategy can be seen even more clearly in his relations with the characters in the novel and with the reader's expectations. *Vanity Fair* has as the subtitle, *A Novel without a Hero,* which indicates that the characters are not regarded as representing an ideal, exemplary form of human conduct, as established by the conventions of the eighteenth-century novel. Instead, the reader's interest is divided between two figures who, despite the contrast in their behavior, can under no circumstances be regarded as complementary or even corrective. For Becky, no price is too high for the fulfillment of her social ambitions; her friend Amelia is simple and sentimental. And so right at the beginning we are told:

> As she is not a heroine, there is no need to describe her person; indeed I am afraid that her nose was rather short than otherwise, and her cheeks a great deal too round and red for a heroine; but her face blushed with rosy health, and her lips with the freshest of smiles, and she had a pair of eyes which sparkled with the brightest and honestest good-humour, except indeed when they filled with tears, and that was a great deal too often; for the silly thing would cry over a dead canary-bird; or over a mouse, that the cat haply had seized upon; or over the end of a novel, were it ever so stupid.

The details of such a description serve only to trivialize those features that were so important in the hero or heroine of the traditional novel. These details give the impression that something significant is being said about the person described, but the succession of clichés, from the round red cheeks and sparkling eyes to the soft-hearted sentimentality, achieve their purpose precisely by depriving the character of its representative nature. But if Amelia is deprived of traditional representative qualities and is not to be regarded as the positive counterpart to the unscrupulous, sophisticated Becky, then the novel denies the reader a basic focal point of orientation. He is prevented from sympathizing with the hero—a process which till now had always provided the nineteenth-century reader with his most important means of access to the events described—as typified by the reaction of a reviewer to Charlotte Brontë's *Jane Eyre:* "We took up *Jane Eyre* one winter's evening, somewhat piqued at the extravagant commendations we had heard, and sternly resolved to be as critical as Croker. But as we read on we forgot both commendations and criticism, identified ourselves with Jane in all her troubles, and finally married Mr. Rochester about four in the morning" (quoted in Kathleen Tillotson, *Novels of the Eighteen-Forties*). In contrast, *Vanity Fair* seems bent on breaking any such direct contact with the characters, and indeed the narrator frequently goes out of his way to prevent the reader from putting himself in their place.

This occurs predominantly through the narrator's comments on the particular patterns of behavior developed by Amelia and Becky in critical situations. He reveals the motives behind their utterances, interpolating consequences of which they themselves are not aware, so that these occasions serve to uncover the imbalance of the characters. Often the behavior of the characters is interpreted far beyond the scope of the reactions shown and in the light of knowledge which at best could only have been revealed by the future. In this way the reader is continually placed at a distance from the characters. As Michel Butor once pointed out, in a different context: "If the reader is put in the place of the hero, he must also be put in the hero's immediate present; he cannot know what the hero does not know, and things must appear to him just as they appear to the hero." In *Vanity Fair,* however, the characters are illuminated by a knowledge to which they themselves have no access. They are constantly kept down below the intellectual level of the narrator, whose views offer the reader a far greater stimulus to identification than do the characters themselves. This detachment from the characters is part of the narrator's avowed intention: "as we bring our characters forward, I will ask leave, as a man and a brother, not only to introduce them, but occasionally to step down from the platform, and talk about them: if they are good and kindly, to love them and shake them by the hand; if they are silly, to laugh at them confidentially in the reader's sleeve: if they are wicked and heartless, to abuse them in the strongest terms which politeness admits of." The characters in this novel are completely hedged in by such judgments, and the reader sees all their actions only when they have been refracted by the narrator's own critical evaluations. The immensity of his presence makes it impossible for the reader to live their lives with them, as did the reviewer we have quoted, during his reading of *Jane Eyre*. The actual gap between the characters' actions and the narrator's comments stimulates the reader into forming judgments of his own— thereby bridging the gaps—and gradually adopting the position of critic himself.

It is mainly this intention that shapes the composition of the characters, and there are two dominant techniques to be observed. The first part of the novel reproduces letters which Becky and Amelia write to each other. The letter makes it possible to reveal the most intimate thoughts and feelings to such a degree that the reader can learn from the correspondents themselves just who they are and what makes them "tick." A typical example is Becky's long letter telling Amelia all about her new surroundings at the Crawley family's country seat. Becky's impressions end with the spontaneous self-revelation: "I am determined to make myself agreeable." Fitting in with present circumstances remains her guiding principle throughout her quest for social advancement. Such a wish is so totally in keeping with her own character that the maneuvers necessary for its fulfillment constitute for Becky the natural way to behave. Thus we see that in society, self-seeking hypocrisy has become second nature to man. In the letters, however, Becky's self-esteem remains so constant that she is clearly quite unaware of her two-facedness. The obvious naïveté of such self-portraits is bound to provoke the reader into critical reaction, and the heading of the chapter that reproduces Becky's letter is already pointing in this direction, for the unmistakably ironic title is "Arcadian Simplicity." Thus the self-revelation of the letter actually justifies the narrator for not taking the character as it is, but setting it at a critical distance so that it can be seen through. Elsewhere we read: "Perhaps in Vanity Fair there are no better satires than letters." But the intention of the satire is for the reader himself to uncover, for the narrator never offers him more than ironic clues. The narrator's keen concern to give the impression that he never commits himself to ultimate clarity reveals itself at those times when he accidentally reaches an "understanding" with his reader, but then remembers that such an exchange of experiences goes beyond the limits of his narrative: "but we are wandering out of the domain of the story."

The second technique designed to rouse the critical faculties of the reader is revealed in Amelia's almost obsessive habit of "building numberless castles in the air . . . which Amelia adorned with all sorts of flower-gardens, rustic walks, country churches, Sunday schools, and the like." This day-dreaming is typical of Amelia, who devises these beautiful visions as an escape from the narrow confines of her social existence. Her whole outlook is governed by expectations that generally arise out of chance events in her life and are therefore as subject to fortuitous change as the social situations she gets into. The dependence of these often very sentimental day-dreams on the circumstances of the moment shows not only the fickleness of her behavior but also the disorientated nature of her desires, the fulfillment of which is inevitably frustrated by the apparently superior forces of her environment. The projection of hopes which cannot be realized leads to an attitude which is as characteristic of Amelia as it is of Becky, who for different motives also covers up what she really is, in order to gain the social position she hankers after. Despite the difference in their motives, both Amelia's and Becky's lives are largely governed by illusions, which are shown up for what they are by the fact that whenever they are partially realized, we see how very trivial the aspirations really were. The characters themselves, however, lack this awareness, and this is hardly surprising, as their ambitions or longings are often roused by chance occurrences which are not of sufficient lasting importance to give the characters a true sense of direction. Becky certainly has greater drive in her quest for social advancement, and one would therefore expect a greater degree of continuity in her conduct; but this very ambition requires that she should adapt her conduct to the various demands made by the different strata of society; and this fact in turn shows how malleable and therefore illusory are the conventions of social life. What is presented in Becky's life as continuity should not be confused with the aspirations of the eighteenth-century hero, who went forth in order to find out the truth about himself; here it is the expression of the many-sided sham which is the very attribute of social reality.

When the narrator introduces his characters at the beginning of the novel, he says of Becky: "The famous little Becky Puppet has been pronounced to be uncommonly flexible in the joints, and lively on the wire." As the characters cannot free themselves from their illusions, it is only to be expected that they should take them for unquestionable reality. The reader is made aware of this fact by the attitude of the narrator, who has not only seen through his "puppets," but also lets them act on a level of consciousness far below his own. This almost overwhelming superiority of the narrator over his characters also puts the reader in a privileged position, though with the unspoken but ever-present condition that he should draw his own conclusions from the extra knowledge imparted to him by the narrator. There is even an allegory of the reader's task at one point in the novel, when Becky is basking in the splendor of a grand social evening:

> The man who brought her refreshment and stood behind her chair, had talked her character over with the large gentleman in motley-coloured clothes at his side. Bon Dieu! it is awful, that servants' inquisition! You see a woman in a great party in a splendid saloon, surrounded by faithful admirers, distributing sparkling glances, dressed to perfection, curled, rouged, smiling and happy:—Discovery walks respectfully up to her, in the shape of a huge powdered man with large calves and a tray of ices—with Calumny (which is as fatal as truth) behind him, in the shape of the hulking fellow carrying the wafer-biscuits, Madam, your secret will be talked over by those men at their club at the public-house to-night. . . . Some people ought to have mutes for servants in Vanity Fair—mutes who could not write. If you are guilty, tremble. That fellow behind your chair may be a Janissary with a bowstring in his plush breeches pocket. If you are not guilty, have a care of appearances: which are as ruinous as guilt.

This little scene contains a change of standpoints typical of the way in which the reader's observations are conditioned throughout this novel. The servants are suddenly transformed into allegorical figures with the function of uncovering what lies hidden beneath the façades of their masters. But the discovery will only turn into calumny from the standpoint of the person affected. The narrator compares the destructive effect of calumny with that of truth and advises his readers to employ mutes, or better still illiterate mutes, as servants, in order to protect themselves against discovery. Then he brings the reader's view even more sharply into focus, finally leaving him to himself with an indissoluble ambiguity: if he feels guilty, because he is pretending to be something he is not, then he must fear those around him as if they were an army of Janissaries. If he has nothing to hide, then the social circle merely demands of him to keep up appearances; but since this is just as ruinous as deliberate hypocrisy, it follows that life in society imposes roles on all concerned, reducing human behavior to the level of play-acting. All the characters in the novel are caught up in this play, as is expressly shown by the narrator's own stage metaphor at the beginning and at the end. The key word for the reader is "discover," and the narrator continually prods him along the road to discovery, laying a trail of clues for him to follow. The process reveals not only the extent to which Becky and Amelia take their illusions for reality but also—even more strikingly—the extent to which reality itself is illusory, since it is built on the simulated relationships between people. The reader will not fail to notice the gulf between "illusion" and "reality," and in realizing it, he is experiencing the esthetic effect of the novel: Thackeray did not set out to create the conventional illusion that involved the reader in the world of the novel as if it were reality; instead, his narrator constantly interrupts the story precisely in order to prevent such an illusion from coming into being. The reader is deliberately stopped from identifying himself with the characters. And as the aim is to prevent him from taking part in the events, he is allowed to be absorbed only to a certain degree and is then jerked back again, so that he is impelled to criticize from the outside. Thus the story of the two girls serves to get the reader involved, while the meaning of the story can only be arrived at by way of the additional manipulations of perspective carried out by the narrator.

This "split-level" technique conveys a far stronger impression of reality than does the illusion which claims that the world of the novel corresponds to the whole world. For now the reader himself has to discover the true situation, which becomes clearer and clearer to him as he gets to know the characters in their fetters of illusion. In this way, he himself takes an active part in the animation of all the characters' actions, for they seem real to him because he is constantly under obligation to work out all that is wrong with their behavior. In order that his participation should not be allowed to slacken, the individual characters are fitted out with different types and degrees of delusion, and there are even some, like Dobbin, whose actions and feelings might mislead one into taking them for positive counterparts to all the other characters. Such a false assumption is certainly perceived, even if not intended, by the narrator, who toward the end of the novel addresses the reader as follows: "This woman [i.e., Amelia] had a way of tyrannising over Major Dobbin (for the weakest of all people will domineer over somebody), and she ordered him about, and patted him, and made him fetch and carry just as if he was a great Newfoundland dog. . . . This history has been written to very little purpose if the reader has not perceived that the Major was a spooney." What might have seemed like noble-mindedness was in fact the behavior of a nincompoop, and if the reader has only just realized it, then he has not been particularly successful in the process of "discovering."

The esthetic effect of *Vanity Fair* depends on activating the reader's critical faculties so that he may recognize the social reality of the novel as a confusing array of sham attitudes, and experience the exposure of this sham as the true reality. Instead of being expressly stated, the criteria for such judgments have to be inferred. They are the blanks which the reader is supposed to fill in, thus bringing his own criticism to bear. In other words, it is his own criticism that constitutes the reality of the book. The novel, then, is not to be viewed as the mere reflection of a social reality, for its true form will only be revealed when the world it presents has, like all images, been refracted and converted by the mind of the reader. *Vanity Fair* aims not at presenting social reality, but at presenting the way in which such reality can be experienced. "To convey as strongly as possible the sentiment of reality" is Thackeray's description of this process, which he regarded as the function of the novel. If the sense of the narrative can only be completed through the cooperation of the reader (which is allowed for in the text), then the borderline between fiction and reality becomes increasingly hazy, for the reader can scarcely regard his own participation as fictional. He is bound to look on his reactions as something real, and at no time is this conviction disputed. But since his reactions are real, he will lose the feeling that he is judging a world that is only fictional. Indeed, his own judgments will enhance the impression he has that this world is a reality.

How very concerned Thackeray was to confront the reader with a reality he himself considered to be real is clear from the passage already quoted, in which the narrator tells the reader that his object is to walk with him through the Fair and leave him "perfectly miserable" afterward. Thackeray reiterates this intention in a letter written in 1848: "my object . . . is to indicate, in cheerful terms, that we are for the most part an abominably foolish and selfish people . . . all eager after vanities . . . I want to leave everybody dissatisfied and unhappy at the end of the story—we ought all to be with our own and all other stories." For this insight to take root in the reader, the fictional world must be made to seem real to him. Since, in addition, the reader is intended to be a critic of this world, the esthetic appeal of the novel lies in the fact that it gives him the opportunity to step back and take a detached look at that which he had regarded as normal human conduct. This detachment, however, is not to be equated with the edification which the moral novel offered to its readers. Leaving the reader perfectly miserable after his reading indicates that such a novel is not going to offer him pictures of another world that will make him forget the sordid nature of this one; the reader is forced, rather, to exercise his own critical faculties in order to relieve his distress by uncovering potential alternatives arising out of the world he has read about. "A man with a reflective turn of mind" is therefore the ideal reader for this novel. W. J. Harvey has remarked, in a different context:

> A novel . . . can allow for a much fuller expression of this sensed penumbra of unrealized possibilities, of all the what-might-have-beens of our lives. It is because of this that the novel permits a much greater liberty of such speculation on the part of the reader than does the play. Such speculation frequently becomes, as it does in real life, part of the substantial reality of the identity of any character. The character moves in the full depth of his conditional freedom; he is what he is but he might have been otherwise. Indeed the novel does not merely *allow* for this liberty of speculation; sometimes it *encourages* it to the extent that our sense of conditional freedom in this aspect becomes one of the ordering structual principles of the entire work.
>
> (*Character and the Novel*)

IV

The aspect of the novel which we have discussed so far is the narrator's continual endeavor to stimulate the reader's mind through extensive commentaries on the actions of the characters. This indirect form of guidance is supplemented by a number of remarks relating directly to the expectations and supposed habits of the novel-reader. If the fulfillment of the novel demands a heightened faculty of judgment, it is only natural that the narrator should also compel the reader—at times quite openly—to reflect on his own situation, for without doing so he will be incapable of judging the actions of the characters in the novel. For this process to be effective, the possible reader must be visualized as playing a particular role with particular characteristics, which may vary according to circumstances. And so just as the author divides himself up into the narrator of the story and the commentator on the events in the story, the reader is also stylized to a certain degree, being given attributes which he may either accept or reject. Whatever happens he will be forced to react to those ready-made qualities ascribed to him. In this manner the double role of the author has a parallel in that of the reader, as W. Booth has pointed out in a discussion on the narrator:

> The same distinction must be made between myself as reader and the very often different self who goes about paying bills, repairing leaky faucets, and failing in generosity and wisdom. It is only as I read that I become the self whose beliefs must coincide with the author's. Regardless of my real beliefs and practices, I must subordinate my mind and heart to the book if I am to enjoy it to the full. The author creates, in short, an image of himself and another image of his reader; he makes his reader, as he makes his second self, and the most successful reading is one in which the created selves, author and reader, can find complete agreement.
>
> (*The Rhetoric of Fiction*)

Such an agreement can, however, be reached along widely differing lines, for instance through disagreement—i.e., a subtly instituted opposition between reader and narrator—and this is what happens in *Vanity Fair*.

When the narrator pretends to be at one with the reader in evaluating a certain situation, the reverse is usually the case. For instance, he describes an old but rich spinster who is a member of the great Crawley family, into which Becky is going to marry, in fulfillment of her social aspirations:

> Miss Crawley was . . . an object of great respect when she came to Queen's Crawley, for she had a balance at her banker's which would have made her beloved anywhere. What a dignity it gives an old lady, that balance at the banker's! How tenderly we look at her faults if she is a

relative (and may every reader have a score of such), what a kind good-natured old creature we find her! . . . How, when she comes to pay us a visit, we generally find an opportunity to let our friends know her station in the world! We say (and with perfect truth) I wish I had Miss MacWhirter's signature to a cheque for five thousand pounds. She wouldn't miss it, says your wife. She is my aunt, say you, in an easy careless way, when your friend asks if Miss MacWhirter is any relative. Your wife is perpetually sending her little testimonies of affection, your little girls work endless worsted baskets, cushions, and footstools for her. What a good fire there is in her room when she comes to pay you a visit, although your wife laces her stays without one! . . . Is it so, or is it not so?

By using the first-person plural, the narrator gives the impression that he is viewing through the reader's eyes the many attentions paid to the old lady with the large bank balance; for the reader such conduct is scarcely remarkable—indeed it is more the expression of a certain *savoir vivre*. By identifying himself with this view, the narrator seems to reinforce rather than to oppose this attitude, which is symptomatic of human nature. But in pretending merely to be describing "natural" reactions, he is in fact seeking to trap the reader into agreeing with him—and as soon as that is accomplished, the reader realizes for himself the extent to which consideration of personal gain shapes the natural impulses of human conduct.

In this way, the difference between the reader and the characters in the novel is eliminated. Instead of just seeing through them, he sees himself reflected in them, so that the superior position which the narrator has given him over the pretences and illusions of the characters now begins to fade. The reader realizes that he is similar to those who are supposed to be the objects of his criticism, and so the self-confrontations that permeate the novel compel him to become aware of his own position in evaluating that of the characters. In order to develop this awareness, the narrator creates situations in which the characters' actions correspond to what the reader is tricked into regarding as natural, subsequently feeling the irresistible urge to detach himself from the proceedings. And if the reader ignores the discreet summons to observe himself, then his critical attitude toward the characters becomes unintentionally hypocritical, for he forgets to include himself in the judgment. Thackeray did not want to edify his readers, but to leave them miserable, though with the tacit invitation to find ways of changing this condition for themselves.

This predominantly intellectual appeal to the mind of the reader was not always the norm in the realistic novel. In Dickens, for example, emotions are aroused in order to create a premeditated relationship between the reader and the characters. A typical illustration of this is the famous scene at the beginning of *Oliver Twist,* when the hungry child in the workhouse has the effrontery (as the narrator sees it) to ask for another plate of soup. In the presentation of this daring exploit, Oliver's inner feelings are deliberately excluded, in order to give greater emphasis to the indignation of the authorities at such an unreasonable request. The narrator comes down heavily on the side of authority, and can thus be quite sure that his hard-hearted attitude will arouse a flood of sympathy in his readers for the poor starving child. The reader is thus drawn so far into the action that he feels he must interfere. This effect, not unlike the tension at a Punch and Judy show, enables Dickens to convey contemporary reality to his readers. He follows traditional practice insofar as he brings about a total involvement of the reader in the action. In Thackeray things are different. He is concerned with preventing any close liaison between reader and characters. The reader of *Vanity Fair* is in fact forced into a position outside the reality of the novel, though the judgment demanded of him is not without a tension of its own, as he is always in danger of sliding into the action of the novel, thereby suddenly being subjected to the standards of his own criticism.

The narrator does not aim exclusively at precipitating his reader into such situations of involuntary identification with the characters. In order to sharpen the critical gaze, he also offers other modes of approach, though these demand a certain effort at discrimination on the part of the reader—for instance, when he wishes to describe, at least indirectly, the various aspects of the important love affair between Amelia and Osborne:

> The observant reader, who has marked our young Lieutenant's previous behaviour, and has preserved our report of the brief conversation which he has just had with Captain Dobbin, has possibly come to certain conclusions regarding the character of Mr. Osborne. Some cynical Frenchman has said that there are two parties to a love-

transaction: the one who loves and the one who conde-
scends to be so treated. Perhaps the love is occasionally on
the man's side; perhaps on the lady's. Perhaps some infatuated swain has ere this mistaken insensibility for mod-
esty, dullness for maiden reserve, mere vacuity for sweet
bashfulness, and a goose, in a word, for a swan. Perhaps
some beloved female subscriber has arrayed an ass in the
splendour and glory of her imagination; admired his dullness as manly simplicity; worshipped his selfishness as
manly superiority; treated his stupidity as majestic gravity,
and used him as the brilliant fairy Titania did a certain
weaver at Athens. I think I have seen such comedies of
errors going on in the world. But this is certain, that Amelia
believed her lover to be one of the most gallant and brilliant men in the empire: and it is possible Lieutenant
Osborne thought so too.

Apparently simple situations are taken apart for the reader and split
up into different facets. He is free to work his way through each one
and to choose whichever he thinks most appropriate, but whether
this decision favor the image of the cynical Frenchman or that of the
infatuated swain, there will always remain an element of doubt over
the relationship under discussion. Indeed the definite view that Amelia
has of her relationship with Osborne acts as a warning to the reader,
as such a final, unambiguous decision runs the risk of being wrong.
    The reader is constantly forced to think in terms of alternatives,
as the only way in which he can avoid the unambiguous and suspect
position of the characters is to visualize the possibilities which they
have not thought of. While he is working out these alternatives the
scope of his own judgment expands, and he is constantly invited to
test and weigh the insights he has arrived at as a result of the pro-
fusion of situations offered him. The esthetic appeal of such a technique consists in the fact that it allows a certain latitude for the
individual character of the reader, but also compels specific reactions—often unobtrusively—without expressly formulating them.
By refusing to draw the reader into the illusory reality of the novel,
and keeping him at a variable distance from the events, the text gives
him the illusion that he can judge the proceedings in accordance with
his own point of view. To do this, he has only to be placed in
a position that will provoke him to pass judgments, and the

less loaded in advance these judgments are by the text, the greater will be the esthetic effect.

The "Manager of the Performance" opens up a whole panorama of views on the reality described, which can be seen from practically every social and human standpoint. The reader is offered a host of different perspectives, and so is almost continually confronted with the problem of how to make them consistent. This is all the more complicated as it is not just a matter of forming a view of the social world described, but of doing so in face of a rich variety of viewpoints offered by the commentator. There can be no doubt that the author wants to induce his reader to assume a critical attitude toward the reality portrayed, but at the same time he gives him the alternative of adopting one of the views offered him, or of developing one of his own. This choice is not without a certain amount of risk. If the reader adopts one of the attitudes suggested by the author, he must automatically exclude the others. If this happens, the impression arises, in this particular novel, that one is looking more at oneself than at the event described. There is an unmistakable narrowness in every standpoint, and in this respect the reflection the reader will see of himself will be anything but complimentary. But if the reader then changes his viewpoint, in order to avoid this narrowness, he will undergo the additional experience of finding that his behavior is very like that of the two girls who are constantly adapting themselves in order to ascend the social scale. All the same, his criticism of the girls appears to be valid. Is it not a reasonable assumption then that the novel was constructed as a means of turning the reader's criticism of social opportunism back upon himself? This is not mentioned specifically in the text, but it happens all the time. Thus, instead of society, the reader finds himself to be the object of criticism.

V

Thackeray once mentioned casually: "I have said somewhere it is the unwritten part of books that would be the most interesting." It is in the unwritten part of the book that the reader has his place—hovering between the world of the characters and the guiding sovereignty of the "Manager of the Performance." If he comes too close to the characters, he learns the truth of what the narrator told him at the beginning: "The world is a looking-glass, and gives back to every man the reflection of his own face." If he stands back with the narrator to look at things from a distance, he sees through all the activities of the characters. Through the variableness of his own position, the reader experiences the meaning of *Vanity Fair*. Through the characters he undergoes a temporary entanglement in the web of his own illusions, and through the demand for judgment he is enabled to free himself from it and to get a better view of himself and of the world.

And so the story of the two girls and their social aspirations forms only one aspect of the novel, which is continually supplemented by views through different lenses, all of which are trained on the story with the intention of discovering its meaning. The necessity for these different perspectives indicates that the story itself does not reveal direct evidence as to its meaning, so that the factual reality depicted does not represent a total reality. It can only become total through the *manner* in which it is observed. Thus the narrator's commentary, with its often ingenious provocations of the reader, has the effect of an almost independent action running parallel to the story itself. Herein lies the difference between Thackeray and the naturalists of the nineteenth century, who set out to convince their readers that a relevant "slice of life" was total reality, whereas in fact it only represented an ideological assumption which, for all the accuracy of its details, was a manipulated reality.

In *Vanity Fair* it is not the slice of life, but the means of observing it that constitute the reality, and as these means of observation remain as valid today as they were in the nineteenth century, the novel remains as "real" now as it was then, even though the social world depicted is only of historical interest. It is in the preoccupation with different perspectives and with the activation of the reader himself that *Vanity Fair* marks a stage of transition between the traditional and what we now call the "modern" novel. The predominant aim is no longer to create the illusion of an objective outside reality, and the novelist is no longer concerned with projecting his own unambiguous view of the world onto his reader. Instead, his technique is to diversify his vision, in order to compel the reader to view things for himself and to discover his own reality. The author has not yet withdrawn "to pare his fingernails," but he has already entered into the shadows and holds his scissors at the ready.

Vision and Satire: The Warped Looking Glass in *Vanity Fair*

Robert E. Lougy

> *The more complex a vision the less it lends itself to satire: the more it*
> *understands the less it is able to sum up and make linear.*
> VIRGINIA WOOLF, *A Writer's Diary,* 6 May 1935

Thackeray introduces us into his novel with a metaphor of the fair or
carnival, a metaphor, it seems, intended to embody Thackeray's
perception both of the novel and of the world it depicts. But because
Thackeray's vision of the world he is creating undergoes strange
transformations, this fair changes before our eyes as we are led
through it. When we first enter the fair, Thackeray is its manager,
exhibiting before us a creation of his own making, one he understands and thus is able to control. However, we are not far into it
before we realize that we are witnessing the unfolding of an artistic
vision at once more profound and more frightening than even its
creator may have anticipated, and consequently one that Thackeray
is at times barely able either to comprehend or to control. For if
Thackeray's original conception of *Vanity Fair* was an admirable one,
it was also one predicated upon certain assumptions that were to
become increasingly difficult for him to believe in as the novel
evolved. These assumptions are most pervasive in the novel's earlier
sections, in which we see a vision belonging to comedy insofar as it
reaffirms a faith in society and in man as social being and to moral
and social satire insofar as it defends the power of laughter in helping

From *PMLA* 90, no. 2 (March 1975). © 1975 by the Modern Language Association
of America.

man to rid himself of his own pretenses and follies and society of at least some of its ills.

But as it unfolds, *Vanity Fair* seems to turn against its initial thrusts, not only by calling into question the efficacy of laughter as an artistic device, but also by undermining its own original faith in society. The consequent tensions and anxieties created by this change are seen quite early in *Vanity Fair*—in fact, as early as Thackeray's own title-page illustration to the novel. In the illustration's foreground is Thackeray's "friend in motley," sitting on a plank stage, resting his shoulders against an opened stage trunk, a wooden sword by his side. Dressed in rather tattered clothing, he is gazing into a mirror in his right hand. He grips the mirror by the frame rather than by the handle, as if he had intended to pick it up for just a moment; his gaze, however, is so steady and so intense that we must believe he has been gazing into the mirror for quite a while, either at something new or at a rediscovery of something old. But for whatever reason he may have picked up the mirror, his original intentions now seem frozen in time in a permanently suspended gesture. The whole foreground consists of such tensions: the player's position of apparent physical relaxation is belied by his tired and melancholic expression and by the intensity of his stare into the mirror; and his disheveled appearance and facial features deny him the appearance of either the clown or the soldier—Thackeray's player is neither comic nor heroic.

In fact, tension seems to pervade the whole illustration. An almost concealed section of split-rail fence separates the player and the stage from the shaded background, and in the distance is a gothic cathedral surrounded by dwellings which are themselves almost hidden by thick clusters of foliage. Within the illustration, we see two Englands suspended in space: in the foreground is the stage and on it, the nonheroic soldier, the noncomic buffoon; in the background is a strong and serene England, one of gothic architecture, cottages, and protective trees. These two worlds are divided by a meager split-rail fence, but one feels that this barrier will suffice. This sense of two disparate worlds also characterizes the novel itself, with the pastoral or private vision in the background, set off against the predominant world of facade, loneliness, and alienation. Within the novel, Thackeray's pastoral is always present, although much of the time submerged, and it asserts itself most powerfully only after Thackeray has worked his way through—and beyond—the novel's other major and more traditional motifs or impulses. It is in this respect that *Vanity Fair* ends where it begins, with Thackeray simultaneously aware of this distant pastoral vision and of his exclusion from it.

I

One of *Vanity Fair*'s major motifs, while its most obvious and pervasive, is also the novel's clearest example of an inherited tradition Thackeray was to move beyond before he could respond to the world he saw: "Ah! *Vanitas Vanitatum!* Which of us is happy in this world? Which of us has his desire? or, having it, is satisfied?" (chap. 67). Beneath the surface hilarity and gaiety of *Vanity Fair* is an omnipresent death's-head, a reminder of that identical end toward which all life moves; but as symbol the death's-head is isolated in *Vanity Fair* in a way that it is not, for example, in *Pilgrim's Progress* or *Everyman*. Bunyan and the author of *Everyman* establish it within the context of a Christian world view that allows us to accompany their heroes to a higher structure of values and beliefs which depend largely upon our recognition of the transience of this world's goods. We begin with a limited knowledge, perceiving its inadequacies only after we witness our own mortality in Christian's or Everyman's experiences. Such knowledge is potentially redemptive because it makes us aware of the superiority of the eternal over the transient, the sacred over the profane. To be shown the limitations of this world, however, at the same time that we are deprived of the certainty of the next leads to another sort of wisdom than Bunyan had in mind.

In FitzGerald's *The Rubáiyát of Omar Khayyám*, one of the classic nineteenth-century expressions of this particular wisdom, the speaker chooses to "make the most of what we yet may spend, / Before we too in the Dust descend." This is, of course, precisely the position that Christian and Everyman learn to reject as an absurd—and damning—proposition. Yet Thackeray, closer in many respects to FitzGerald than to Bunyan, is at one point in *Vanity Fair* led to a similar observation:

It is all vanity to be sure: but who will not own to liking a little of it? I should like to know what well-constituted mind, merely because it is transitory, dislikes roast-beef? That is a vanity; but may every man who reads this, have

> a wholesome portion of it through life. . . . Yes, let us eat
> our fill of the vain thing, and be thankful therefor.
>
> (Chap. 51)

But such a statement leads him into predictable difficulties, for if we
are to be thankful for "our fill" of vain things, then we should "make
the best of Becky's aristocratic pleasures likewise—for these too,
like all other mortal delights, were but transitory" (chap. 51). The
death's-head renders values and priorities meaningless, unless there is
a promise—absent in *Vanity Fair*—of a world to follow. Roast beef
and aristocratic pleasures are equally futile and equally satisfactory
responses to the physical world if, by definition, all is vain; if all
mortal delights are transitory, no one delight can be either better or
worse than another. Thackeray, however, does not admit so quickly
to the truth of such a proposition, and another of *Vanity Fair*'s motifs, the satiric, prevents us also from drawing such a conclusion too
hastily.

Thackeray's "friend in motley," regarding himself in a mirror,
is both the object and the spectator of satire. By holding a mirror up
to human nature, the satirist allows man to perceive his own foibles
and the degree to which he falls short of that vision of man beyond
his own immediate reflection. *Vanity Fair*'s objects of ridicule are
fairly standard ones—hypocrisy, greed, social climbing, pretense,
moral blindness—and insofar as he holds these failings up to deri-
sion, Thackeray is within an established tradition. Satire runs counter
to the *Vanitas Vanitatum* theme in that it recognizes a priority of
mundane values and attests to man's capacity to understand and,
more important, to act in accordance with his understanding of moral
priorities. Rejecting the notion that all worldly things are equally
vain, satire affirms the belief that man, if shown himself in a true
light, can move from ignorance and moral blindness toward wisdom
and self-knowledge. Yet, as readers have pointed out, we are never
quite sure of the objective of satire in *Vanity Fair*. Few of its characters move from ignorance to knowledge, and, even if they seem
to, such a move does not produce any permanent change in their
values or actions. Satire, no less than tragedy, implies the possibility
of growth and change, and it is this possibility that seems to be
missing in *Vanity Fair*.

Rawdon Crawley's fate can possibly help us see what happens,
in part, to *Vanity Fair*'s satiric impulses. Our increasing sympathy as

readers toward Rawdon parallels a corresponding growth of sympathy on Thackeray's own part. Perhaps Thackeray originally conceived of Rawdon only as the hard-living and not overly bright soldier-husband of Becky Sharp; but by the time he departs for almost certain death on Coventry Island, he has become an individual who is, given the right circumstances, capable of great affection and courage. But with his growth—as husband, father, and man—he is increasingly isolated, until finally he is burdened with feelings that must remain private if they are to survive. The only person in whom Rawdon can confide is his sister-in-law, Lady Jane, and he would, we are told, "sit for long hours . . . and talk to her about the virtues, and good looks, and hundred good qualities of the child" (chap. 52). After his release from jail, however, his experiences are such that they cannot be shared, even with her: " 'Oh,' said he, in his rude, artless way, 'you—you don't know how I'm changed since I've known you, and—and little Rawdy. I—I'd like to change somehow. You see I want—I want—to be—' " (chap. 53).

Fulfillment of the self, Rawdon discovers, is not attainable within the public order of Vanity Fair, and thus his exile is but the logical and necessary extension of an alienation already effected. Of all *Vanity Fair*'s characters, Rawdon's experiences most closely resemble those of a religious or heroic nature—his temptations, his temporary fall, his isolation (his night in jail) and his consequently gained wisdom. But after having depicted him struggling to this point, Thackeray correctly chooses permanent exile as the only course of action available to Rawdon. One sees a similar pattern of experience in *Tom Jones* in that both Tom Jones and Rawdon reach the nadir of their existence in jail and emerge from it with discoveries about themselves and their place within their respective worlds. The consequences of this knowledge, however, are profoundly different: Tom Jones moves toward a reintegration within a society made whole by his regained identity and by his reaffirmed love; Rawdon leaves for a disease-ridden island from which he will not return. And along with the departure of this man, disillusioned, alienated, and yet at the true moral center of the novel, *Vanity Fair* moves away from the satiric mode in that wisdom, courage, and love are implicitly denied redemptive powers within its world.

The novel's plot does not in itself require Rawdon's exile to be permanent and unrewarding; one can imagine a number of ways in which Thackeray could have brought Rawdon home, not to a reconciliation with Becky, but to a reunion with his son and Lady Jane. What does require it is Thackeray's evolving vision of society, for by the time Rawdon finally departs, Thackeray is no longer indicting a particular society located within a specific time and place, but is examining the diseased structure of civilization itself. Early in *Vanity Fair* the looking glass is alluded to as an instrument that offers a truly equitable reflection and is, as such, a symbol of the world writ small: "The world is a looking-glass, and gives back to every man the reflection of his own face. Frown at it, and it will in turn look sourly upon you; laugh at it and with it, and it is a jolly kind companion" (chap. 2). Implicit in this metaphor are certain assumptions about the world that Thackeray finds increasingly difficult to believe in—first, that there is a just relationship between one's actions and the consequences reaped from them and, second, that one may gain a certain wisdom in this world, if only the knowledge that the way one is treated by the world depends largely upon the self one presents to it. Such assumptions accommodate satire because they affirm man's capacity to seek wisdom within a world that makes the quest worthwhile. To expose folly, deceit, and humbug is to clear away the diseased underbrush from an otherwise healthy landscape, and Thackeray's use of the metaphor of the looking glass in this passage implies the potential, at least, for satire to move through itself into comedy.

But his use of this particular metaphor changes:

> I want to leave everybody dissatisfied and unhappy at the end of the story [*Vanity Fair*]—we ought all to be with our own and all other stories. Good God dont I see (in that may-be cracked and warped looking glass in which I am always looking) my own weaknesses wickednesses lusts follies short-comings? . . . We must lift up our voices about these and howl to a congregation of fools: so much at least has been my endeavour.
>
> (*Letters*)

As the respective tones of these two passages suggest, the change is profound. In the former, the tone is light, buoyant, almost arrogantly self-assured; in the latter, it is the confessional tone of an angry and disheartened man. And while Thackeray is not wholly certain which mirror truly reflects a just image, referring ambivalently to his "may-be cracked and warped looking glass," it is this latter metaphor that compels his attention and deepest artistic energies. In it, he sees reflected a vision of man beyond the reaches of social, esthetic, or political grace, with the artist no longer the satirist guiding man to wisdom and self-knowledge, but one of the damned howling down sermons to the mad: the artist, because he is an artist, must still howl, but in a manner more akin to Céline than to Fielding.

Such a vision could not have developed without manifesting consequent anxieties and tensions within the novel; and in one ironic passage, fairly late in the novel, we see such manifestations:

> If we are to be peering into everybody's private life, speculating upon their income, and cutting them if we don't approve of their expenditure—why, what a howling wilderness and intolerable dwelling Vanity Fair would be. Every man's hand would be against his neighbour in this case, my dear sir, and the benefits of civilisation would be done away with. We should be quarrelling, abusing, avoiding one another. Our houses would become caverns: and we should go in rags because we cared for nobody. Rents would go down . . . all the delights of life, I say,— would go to the deuce, if people did but act upon their silly principles, and avoid those whom they dislike and abuse. Whereas, by a little charity and mutual forbearance, things are made to go on pleasantly enough. . . . Thus trade flourishes—civilisation advances: peace is kept.
>
> (Chap. 51)

Passages such as this have caused consternation among Thackeray's readers, in that they seem so directly contrary to the novel's main moral thrust, and have caused some to locate another source, usually the narrator as opposed to the author, to whom such sentiments may be attributed. Authorial consistency, however, is not necessarily an artistic virtue—post-Jamesian criticism notwithstanding—and such a passage becomes intelligible if viewed within the dramatic context of a work of art that, as it changed and grew, forced its creator to confront certain implications absent in the *Vanity Fair* he had conceived of earlier.

When Thackeray writes this passage, late in *Vanity Fair,* his relationship to his novel and to the previous tradition of moral satire has become more complex. At the beginning, his role as artist and moral satirist may not have been an easy one, but it was traditional and nonthreatening: Vanity Fair is a "vain, wicked, foolish place, full of all sorts of humbugs and falsenesses and pretensions" and his task is to "have at them . . . with might and main" (chap. 8), using wit and laughter as his weapons. It is "to combat and expose such as those [quacks, fads] no doubt, that Laughter was made" (chap. 8). The world is neither a moral nor a pleasant place; but it is intelligible and thus the artist's relationship to it can be defined: to bring closer together through his art the world as it presently is and the world as it might be if cleansed of humbug, pretense, and foolishness. But what happens if the moral satirist becomes uncertain about the role of laughter itself, if he begins to realize that laughter can be an anarchic as well as a corrective power? What if behind the facades of illusion and pretense there exists not a solid and healthy structure, but instead an emptiness which is in fact contained and controlled by means of those very facades that laughter might destroy? The fear and confusion raised by such questions are mirrored in the troubled irony of the passage above.

Unlike *Vanity Fair*'s earlier irony that issues forth out of moral certainty and an assertive self-confidence in Thackeray's function as artist, this irony threatens throughout to turn in upon itself. Instead of lacerating a society gone astray and oblivious to its own aberrations, it functions to protect Thackeray from the truth of what he has thus far shown. At the same time, it also undermines, in its ambivalent and convoluted impulses, whatever moral and social stability he may have posited earlier. The distance between the world as it is and as it might be has virtually disappeared, but in a frightening and unexpected way: chaos and anarchy (Thackeray's "howling wilderness") on one hand and civilization on the other have become one. There is no indication that those traditional values alluded to—charity and mutual forbearance—are at all effective in bringing forth a more humane society. Indeed, Thackeray's very use of such words tends to distort them almost beyond recognition. But when such virtues are practiced, as in the case of Raggles, the results are invariably painful. In *Vanity Fair* such virtues are translated into the practical necessity of overlooking the transgressions of others so that one's own transgressions may in turn be overlooked.

Thackeray suggests, albeit through a thin and finally ineffective curtain of irony, that civilization does not depend upon a collectively experienced vision, however imperfectly realized, in which the final meaning of man's individual and shared existence should add up to something more than prosperous tradesmen and stabilized rents; instead, it rests upon a tacitly accepted hypocrisy and aggression. And because laughter and satire cut through and destroy those facades and social forms upon which civilization so precariously rests, they are properly seen as anarchic forces. Thus we see the satirist who, because he sees the dangers of his own satire, has become an apologist in defense of the status quo: "all the delights of life . . . would go to the deuce, if people did but act upon their silly principles, and avoid those whom they dislike and abuse" (chap. 51).

II

Since *Vanity Fair's* publication, its darker aspects have disconcerted its readers. As early as 1848, George Henry Lewes protested about the corrupt world that Thackeray depicts—"in *Vanity Fair,* his greatest work, how little there is to love! The people are all scamps, scoundrels, or humbugs" (*Letters*). And in response to his contemporary reviewers, Thackeray observed that, "you have all of you taken my misanthropy to task—I wish I could myself" (*Letters*). A few years later (1851), Thackeray's description of his art suggests that he might have taken such criticism to heart and that he either misremembered or repressed *Vanity Fair's* bleakness and his own comments while writing it: "The present writers are all employed as by instinct in unscrewing the old framework of society, and get it ready for the Smash. I take a sort of pleasure in my little part in the business and in saying destructive things in a good humoured jolly way" (*Letters*). Thackeray may have begun *Vanity Fair* with such an aim but the world he finally shows elicits neither good humor nor laughter. It is defined by aggression—on the battlefield, in the marketplace, in the drawing room—and while the rules of the game vary, the prizes sought and the prices paid are similar. Thus the novel's central section focuses on the Napoleonic battles, for this war is but the symbolic center of a larger war waged throughout, both within the psyches of its citizens and within a social and physical landscape that reflects their inner strifes and deaths. The victims we remember from *Vanity Fair* are not only George Osborne ("well dead with a ball in his odious bowels" [*Letters*], in Thackeray's memorable, if uncharitable, phrase), but Miss Osborne, "a faded old spinster, broken down by more than forty years of dullness and coarse usage" (chap. 56), and Mr. Sedley, Amelia's father, who, having lost in the high-stakes game of finance, seeks solace by playing at business in a make-believe world where neither success nor defeat is possible. One's memory is haunted by people such as these, who have so fully assimilated the deadly values of the system that they are unable to see the price they pay for their participation.

On *Vanity Fair's* battlefields, the visages of death are many. The nothingness that compels Thackeray's most intense gaze is one that is, in Foucault's phrase, "experienced from within as the continuous and constant form of existence." It is in the history of Gaunt House and its inhabitants (chaps. 47–50), where madness becomes an essential rather than an accidental attribute of the human condition, that we see Thackeray working toward an image that will isolate the dominant impulses of *Vanity Fair* and bring them into sharper focus. For while the identifiably mad in the novel may be confined, the space they occupy is neither more nor less rational than the space inhabited by their confiners. In *Vanity Fair,* the extreme examples of madness are not anomalies, but rather the word of the novel made flesh. George Gaunt, for example, the younger son of Lord Steyne and a promising young diplomat, suddenly begins to act strangely and is "sent off" to Brazil: "But people knew better; he never returned from that Brazil expedition—never died there—never lived there—never was there at all. He was nowhere: he was gone out altogether" (chap. 47). In his fate—isolated, unacknowledged, neither alive nor dead—the madman threatens all, and because society perceives this threat, it copes with the reality of the irrational by denying his existence. Madness radiates outward from Gaunt House; it permeates and defines the world beyond it. Standing in a complementary rather than an antithetical relationship to the "rational" and social impulses within the novel, it represents that moment when the mask falls and reveals the emptiness beneath. As such, it is of greater reality than the world it threatens, realizing at any moment its own ever-present potential contained behind the mask.

During his composition of the Gaunt House chapters, Thackeray wrote that he was "strange to say very late with my work" (*Letters*), and part of his difficulty may be found in the chapters' controlling metaphor, Gaunt House's "mysterious taint of blood." For while this particular metaphor penetrates to the truth of what Thackeray has shown, it also encourages us to look in wrong directions for that truth. It does allow him to locate and isolate those diseased impulses of a civilization that emulates Gaunt House and aspires toward it; and to the extent that the metaphor of madness suggests that the disease pervading Gaunt House—and by implication, the society in which it is set—is a psychic one, it is successful. Yet the madness is not transmitted by aberrant or diseased genes, but by social and economic patterns that at once reflect and perpetuate it: the insanity is both individual and collective, evidenced not only in a singularly doomed family, but in the very society whose values the family embodies. The most damaging madness is to be found in the structures outside the madhouse cell; but in using a metaphor that would have sufficed for an earlier literature (for example, Dickens's use of madness within the interpolated tales of *Pickwick Papers*) in which madness as inherited disease or punishment for a dissolute or evil life becomes a teleological and discriminating secular version of Original Sin or divine wrath, Thackeray belies what he has thus far shown or, at least, pulls up short of fully examining it. But if Thackeray stumbles in looking for a metaphor that would reflect that ambiguous causality in the relationship between self and society, an ambiguity that so fascinated the major British novelists of the nineteenth century, the age itself reflected a similarly ambivalent search, giving birth as it did to both the social sciences and psychoanalysis. In any case, Thackeray shows us a society whose ills are neither genetically nor theologically predestined, one whose dialectic is neither between Grace and Corruption nor between the Rich and the Poor, but between life and death. And madness in *Vanity Fair* symbolizes finally the collapse of this dialectic, representing a collective failure to distinguish between reality and illusion, between life and death. The mirror into which *Vanity Fair* gazes, unlike that magic mirror in *Snow White,* can tell less than the truth.

Thackeray's "may-be cracked and warped looking-glass," however, does not lie, and in sharing its reflected world, Thackeray realized that he was opening himself up to the charge of misanthropy, having observed as early as 1845 the ill reception given to the "comic moralist [who] rushes forward, and takes occasion to tell us that society is diseased" by those persons "who wish to lead an easy life." In *Vanity Fair's* unsettling and searing vision, Thackeray moves toward what must have been a disconcerting kinship with Swift, whom he was later to criticize harshly in his lectures on *The English Humourists of the Eighteenth Century* for being too venomous and misanthropic. (These lectures, however, were attended by, as Thackeray expressed it, "Duchesses and great ladies . . . bishop big-wigs and parliament men" [*Letters*], and the nature of his audience may have encouraged Thackeray to temper candor with mercy and prudence.) Like Swift's Lemuel, Thackeray, in *Vanity Fair,* descends into his own vision of hell: "It is currently reported that even in the very inmost circles, they are no happier than the poor wanderers outside the zone; and Becky, who penetrated into the very centre of fashion, and saw the great George IV. face to face, has owned since that there too was Vanity" (chap. 51). In this context, however, *vanity* is a lame word; and in his later essay, "George the Fourth," Thackeray describes more precisely what it was Becky saw in the King: "you find you have nothing—nothing but a coat and a wig and a mask smiling below it—nothing but a great simulacrum." The King of England has become a shadow hiding behind "silk stock-ings, padding, stays, a coat with frogs and a fur collar." If Gaunt House is a microcosm of the society that surrounds it and aspires toward it, then the royal Court is the apotheosis of such a society. In her pilgrimage, Becky climbs toward Gaunt House and the royal Court, achieves temporarily an appearance at each, and, like the objects of her aspirations, she, too, embodies corruption and death.

In the figure of Becky, Thackeray reaches toward a character who is at once unique and at the same time an embodiment of the diseased world about her. She is *Vanity Fair's* most complex and memorable character, and she seems to stand alone by virtue of her joy, her vitality, and her rebellion. Dorothy Van Ghent, for exam-ple, views Becky as "an individual condensation" of "all the imper-atively aggressive, insanely euphoric impulses of a morally sick civilization," but refers nevertheless to Becky's "delighted exercise in being alive." If, however, we finally see Becky as *Vanity Fair's* embodiment of life, we have walked through Thackeray's carnival mistaking the sham for the true. Although we cheer (as we should) when Becky throws Dr. Johnson's Dictionary out of the coach win-dow, this early gesture is one of Becky's few antisocial acts of re-bellion. Similarly, Becky's artfulness and artistic nature are alluded to a number of times—by Thackeray, by other characters, and by Becky herself—but Becky's best and virtually only work of art is herself. She uses her created image of what she is (or more accu-rately, uses people by means of it) to achieve the image of what she wants to be. Indeed, in this respect, Becky can be seen as *Vanity Fair*'s major anti-artist, in Whitehead's sense of the artist as one who says no, since she stands unopposed to the values of society. Throughout the novel, she is intent on fulfilling herself in terms of a myth that corresponds to and defines the expectations and mores of a diseased civilization. But the price she pays for her assimilation into the society and for her inability to see, as Lord Steyne points out, that "everybody is striving for what is not worth the having" (chap. 48), is indeed high. It costs her a great deal to "live well on nothing a year."

Behind Becky's mask—that of a smiling, vivacious young woman—is what Thackeray saw in King George IV; namely, an emptiness concealed only by an extremely tasking assertion of will. Thackeray makes it clear that such an effort does take its toll: "He [Rawdon] fell asleep after dinner in his chair; he did not see the face opposite to him, haggard, weary, and terrible; it lighted up with fresh candid smiles when he woke" (chap. 52). Later in the novel, Thackeray elaborates upon this brief description in an extended metaphor. It is a long passage, but it deserves to be quoted in full:

> I defy any one to say that our Becky, who has certainly some vices, has not been presented to the public in a perfectly genteel and inoffensive manner. In describing this syren, singing and smiling, coaxing and cajoling, the author, with modest pride, asks his readers all round, has he once forgotten the laws of politeness, and showed the monster's hideous tail above water? No! Those who like may peep down under waves that are pretty transparent, and see it writhing and twirling, diabolically hideous and slimy, flapping amongst bones, or curling round corpses; but above the water line, I ask, has not everything been proper, agreeable, and decorous, and has any the most squeamish immoralist in Vanity Fair a right to cry fie? When, however, the syren disappears and dives below, down among the dead men, the water of course grows turbid over her, and it is labour lost to look into it ever so curiously. They look pretty enough when they sit upon a rock, twanging their harps and combing their hair, and sing, and beckon to you to come and hold the looking-glass; but when they sink into their native element, depend

on it those mermaids are about no good, and we had best
not examine the fiendish marine cannibals, revelling and
feasting on their wretched pickled victims.

(Chap. 64)

After reading this passage, it is hard to hold Thackeray respon-
sible for the praise critics have bestowed upon Becky. Perhaps it is
that world beneath the surface that we protect ourselves from when
we find in Becky Sharp an embodiment of life, joy, and vitality; for
beneath the surface, down among the bones, corpses, and "wretched
pickled victims" is a chaos so threatening that we are warned against
it. At the same time, however, we are advised not to mistake the
surface for the depths. In appeasing that "moral world, that has,
perhaps, no particular objection to vice, but an insuperable repug-
nance to hearing vice called by its proper name" (chap. 64), Thackeray
had at least to feign discretion in his characterization of Becky; but
when we read of the siren's or Becky's "hideous tail" as "writhing
and twirling, diabolically hideous and slimy, flapping amongst bones,
or curling around corpses," we need not be especially subtle to see
that Thackeray is describing a particular sexuality, one that is perverted and employed in the service of death. As a "fiendish marine
cannibal," Becky hides her spiritual and psychological emptiness
behind an alluring facade, but when she turns against others those
forces of destruction within herself, she is indeed "haggard, weary,
and terrible."

The reflected world of the looking glass referred to in the above
passage has become by now even more ambiguous. Thackeray warns
us against mistaking illusion for reality, while at the same time leading us into a world in which we necessarily share and participate in
confusion. Beneath the turbid waters into which the siren dives is a
domain that is "pretty transparent." Indeed, it is the domain of
Gaunt House, of the royal Court, of Vanity Fair itself. Metaphor
becomes symbol and the siren's world is *Vanity Fair's* civilization
wherein sexuality, beauty, and grace become forces of death. Gaston
Bachelard has observed that "in order to achieve grotesqueness, it
suffices to abridge an evolution," and Thackeray, who often displays
a finely developed sense of the grotesque, uses the siren figure—
half-fish and half-woman—to achieve this quality. But what is most
grotesque in *Vanity Fair* is not society's aberrations but its norms,
and what is most frightening is not man's entrapment within his

biological past but his entrapment within a diseased structure of his own making.

Thackeray has shown us this domain before in its other guises and behind its many masks, and if we have not seen it, the fault is not his. The looking glass is lucid, but it reflects an opaque world, murky, obscure, and one within which our previous certainties begin to break down. Early in the novel we witness this world's opacity from the outside; by the time it ends we, too, have become enmeshed in it. The first time that Becky plays the role of Clytemnestra (with Rawdon as her Agamemnon) we stand above the audience which is not sure whether it is witnessing a real or illusory murder:

> Scornfully she [Becky] snatches the dagger out of Aegisthus's hand, and advances to the bed. You see it shining over her head in the glimmer of the lamp, and— and the lamp goes out, with a groan, and all is dark.
>
> The darkness and the scene frightened people. Rebecca performed the part so well, and with such ghastly truth, the spectators were all dumb, until, with a burst, all the lamps of the hall blazed out again, when everybody began to shout applause.
>
> (Chap. 51)

But later we, too, participate in the confusion. We never are certain how Jos Sedley died; although his insurance company suspects foul play, it retreats before the forces of Becky and her lawyers. What we do know, however, is that an illustration very late in the novel, entitled "Becky's second appearance in the character of Clytemnestra," depicts her hiding behind a curtain and holding a sinister-looking phial in her hand, eavesdropping upon Jos Sedley pleading with Dobbin:

> Jos clasped his hands, and cried,—"He [Jos] would go back to India. He would do anything; only he must have time: they mustn't say anything to Mrs. Crawley:—she'd— she'd kill me if she knew it. You don't know what a terrible woman she is," the poor wretch said.
>
> (Chap. 67)

After this scene the lights do not come on for us. There is no dispelling of the darkness and confusion. Whether Becky actually committed murder or simply worried Jos to death is perhaps an

interesting point of speculation, but it is not critical to our understanding either of Becky or of the novel. As the ultimate reduction of
another human being, murder in *Vanity Fair* differs in degree rather
than in kind from other such acts of aggression we have seen
throughout the novel. Grinning ironically, the mask conceals the
final scene involving Jos Sedley; it hides, perhaps, certain facts, but
at the same time it reveals larger truths about *Vanity Fair* that render
such facts extraneous.

III

It is also in part through Becky that Thackeray realizes his at
once brilliant and saddening attempts to define alternatives that might
enable *Vanity Fair*'s world to break free from its inexorable pattern of
death and destruction. The beginnings of Thackeray's quest for such
alternatives are seen in one of *Vanity Fair*'s more grotesque recurring
images, that of the aberrant or perverted manifestation of childhood
in senility, disease, or madness. If Thackeray's use of the siren figure
suggests the phylogenetic origin of the grotesque, then his use of
childhood suggests its ontogenetic origins. The traces of childhood
within the individual are not lost, but instead only remain concealed,
and when they do reappear, they reveal the ways in which childhood
in *Vanity Fair* is mangled and destroyed.

Thackeray transforms the Wordsworthian myth of the child as
father of the man into one in which man, sick or insane, engages in
a horrible and perverse repetition of his childhood. Sir Pitt Crawley
ends his life being cared for and bullied by his maid:

> He would cry and sob—whereupon Hester's face and
> manner, which was always exceedingly bland and gentle
> while her lady was present, would change at once and she
> would make faces at him . . . and twirl his chair away
> from the fire he loved to look at—at which he would cry
> more. For this was all that was left after more than seventy
> years of cunning and struggling, and drinking and schem-
> ing, and sin and selfishness—a whimpering old idiot put in
> and out of bed and cleaned and fed like a baby.
>
> (Chap. 40)

Such a fate, however, is not reserved only for the old or the sinful.
George Gaunt, his body young but his mind ravaged by disease, is

also spoken of as a child, "dragging about a child's toy, or nursing the keeper's baby's doll" (chap. 47), crying if his "wine-and-water" was not strong enough.

Childhood in *Vanity Fair* is not a state of prelapsarian happiness; in *Vanity Fair,* the children, too, are either victimized (like Rawdon Crawley, Jr.) or are at once both victim and victimizer (like George Osborne, Jr.), depending upon how fully they have assimilated the values of the society around them. On the other side of the mirror, however, is another childhood, and like the distant gothic background in the novel's title-page illustration, it is less a state of being than a state of mind, a nostalgia less for youth per se than for what Bachelard has called "the expressions of youth," those attributes that childhood should possess rather than those that it does possess. It is toward these "expressions of youth" that Thackeray moves in his search for values that will stand against the nightmare vision that is *Vanity Fair.* These values are identified early in the novel, in Dobbin's childhood and in Fairy Peribanou's cavern. Dobbin, "apart from the rest of the school, . . . quite lonely, and almost happy . . . had for once forgotten the world, and was away with Sindbad the Sailor in the Valley of Diamonds, or with Prince Ahmed and the Fairy Peribanou in that delightful cavern where the Prince found her, and whither we should all like to make a tour" (chap. 5). Not long after this scene, the outside world intrudes, and Dobbin is called forth to fight a battle in behalf of the young George Osborne, but not before the narrator observes:

> If people would but leave children to themselves; if teachers would cease to bully them; if parents would not insist upon directing their thoughts, and dominating their feelings—those feelings and thoughts which are a mystery to all (for how much do you and I know of each other, of our children, of our fathers, of our neighbour, and how far more beautiful and sacred are the thoughts of the poor lad or girl whom you govern likely to be, than those of the dull and world-corrupted person who rules him?)
>
> (Chap. 5)

This observation and the scene itself establish two distinctive realms. The first is embodied by Dobbin during those moments when he "had for once forgotten the world": a sanctified and solitary realm within which mysterious feelings and thoughts remain inviolate, it is a domain, like those magic lands in *The 1001 Arabian Nights*, where desire and fulfillment merge. But it is protected only by the thinnest of walls and thus is easily violated by the other realm—one of domination and aggression, presided over by teachers and parents, who are embodiments, by virtue of their will to power, of what Thackeray calls the "world-corrupted person." This realm threatens and violates the first, and once it does intrude, its consequences are immediately felt:

> Down came the stump with a great heavy thump on the child's hand. A moan followed. Dobbin looked up. The Princess Peribanou had fled into the inmost cavern with Prince Ahmed: the Roc had whisked away Sindbad the Sailor out of the Valley of Diamonds out of sight, far into the clouds: and there was every-day life before honest William; and a big boy beating a little one without cause.
>
> (Chap. 5)

Our immediate response to such a passage is probably to view what happens to Dobbin as both inevitable and desirable, to see it as the intrusion of reality, "everyday life," into a fantasy realm within which no one can live forever. And while such a response is valid—Dobbin's actions when his reverie is broken do give us some indications of the man he will become—it cannot account for the ambivalence of Thackeray's own attitudes, especially toward the latter part of the novel. For if Thackeray as artist must show the world of *Vanity Fair*, he is at the same time drawn to the figure of young Dobbin, alone, forgetful of the world, and almost happy. Thackeray creates from within his own reveries and visions a world that is intact, self-sustained, and antithetical to that other world he has depicted; and as the vision of *Vanity Fair* evolves more fully and its delineations become even clearer for that artist who had wanted to laugh out of existence those things he later realized could not be destroyed by laughter and, indeed, made laughter impossible, Thackeray returns to the cavern of Fairy Peribanou, "whither we should all like to make a tour." This cavern becomes for him a repository of memories, located in space rather than in time, memories of the "expression of youth," usually relived or recaptured as an adult. When such memories are regained, if only for an instant, they stand apart from and opposed to the present moment and represent a plane of experience more intense and more real than the world of *Vanity Fair* makes possible. But because they also create a heightened awareness of the disparity between the world the person now possesses and the world he or she once loved, these moments evoke a profound sense of loss as well.

For those who return to them, such scenes of reverie or memory, in spite of their various configurations, remain the same land, fulfilling similar needs and desires. There are a number of such passages in *Vanity Fair* and in the first I should like to speak of, the dreamer and wanderer is Lady Steyne, taken back through time by Mozart's music:

> She [Becky] sang religious songs of Mozart, which had been early favourites of Lady Steyne, and with such sweetness and tenderness that the lady lingering round the piano, sate down by its side, and listened until the tears rolled down her eyes. It is true that the opposition ladies at the other end of the room kept up a loud and ceaseless buzzing and talking: but the Lady Steyne did not hear those rumours. She was a child again—and had wandered back through a forty years' wilderness to her Convent Garden. The chapel organ had pealed the same tones, the organist, the sister whom she loved best of the community, had taught them to her in those early happy days. She was a girl once more, and the brief period of her happiness bloomed out again for an hour.
>
> (Chap. 49)

Mozart's music takes Lady Steyne back through time and space, "back through a forty years' wilderness," to a convent garden inhabited by people and sounds representing for her a life that was integrated and whole. Within this garden or visionary world, Lady Steyne, unhappy and alone, like so many of *Vanity Fair*'s characters, forgets the outside world and is "a child again." But like Eurydice, Lady Steyne's momentary escape makes all the more poignant her return to that hell awaiting her. For return to it she must. Her brief reverie is broken—"she started when the jarring doors were flung open, and with a loud laugh from Lord Steyne, the men of the party entered full of gaiety." In the disparity between the quietly weeping Lady Steyne, enclosed by a serenity and self-contained happiness, and the loud laughter and boisterous gaiety of the men who burst into the room, we see once again the radical distinction between those two worlds Thackeray established in his early description of Dobbin. One is a center of peace out of which radiate the sounds of life; the other is a wilderness out of which reverberate the noises of death.

If a reverie through time calls into existence particular and identifiable spaces, so a reverie through certain spaces calls into being a correspondent time. Within *Vanity Fair* are pockets of memory that contain suspended images of warmth and life. Such an image is seen late in the novel, again through the character of Dobbin, but the real traveler here is Thackeray, moving back through time into a garden very much like Lady Steyne's:

> How happy and green the country looked as the chaise whirled rapidly from mile-stone to mile-stone, through neat country towns where landlords came out to welcome him with smiles and bows; by pretty roadside inns, where the signs hung on the elms, and horses and waggoners were drinking under the chequered shadow of the trees; by old halls and parks; rustic hamlets clustered round ancient grey churches—and through the charming friendly English landscape. Is there any in the world like it?
>
> (Chap. 58)

The above scene is so idyllic, so postured, that one can understand why Thackeray has been charged with sentimentality; but such a charge is too easily made and dismisses too many questions too quickly. What calls such a scene into being is the horror of the world Thackeray has been depicting; and he sets against this world an intuited vision of what civilization should be, one that corresponds to Baudelaire's suggestion that "true civilization . . . lies in the reduction of the traces of original sin." Within *Vanity Fair*, two worlds compel Thackeray's attention—the asylum-wilderness and the garden. In the garden is the re-created or recollected past, embodied in England's pastoral youth and in the childhood of the individual.

Bachelard has suggested that "the great function of poetry is to give us back the situation of our dreams" (*The Poetics of Space*), and it is finally this birth into a dream vision that makes it possible for *Vanity Fair*'s characters to forget momentarily the wilderness about them and for Thackeray himself to elicit his own strongest sense of solidity, identity, and beauty. This sense is perhaps seen most clearly in a passage that occurs rather late in the novel:

Fair scenes of peace and sunshine—noble purple mountains, whose crests are reflected in the magnificent stream—
who has ever seen you, that has not a grateful memory of
those scenes of friendly repose and beauty? To lay down
the pen, and even to think of that beautiful Rhineland
makes one happy. At this time of summer evening, the
cows are trooping down from the hills, lowing and with
their bells tinkling, to the old town, with its old moats,
and gates, and spires, and chestnut-trees, with long blue
shadows stretching over the grass; the sky and the river
below flame in crimson and gold; and the moon is already
out, looking pale towards the sunset. The sun sinks behind
the great castle-crested mountains, the night falls suddenly,
the river grows darker and darker, lights quiver in it from
the windows in the old ramparts, and twinkle peacefully in
the villages under the hills on the opposite shore.

(Chap. 62)

Here, as in similar passages, neither Thackeray's imagery nor his
language is original. But, as image, the world brought forth in it is
very real indeed, if we can measure its reality by how fully it occupies an imaginative realm characterized by "friendly repose and
beauty." It is a world of memory, not of fact, that Thackeray creates
for himself—and only secondarily for us—and as the passage itself
suggests, it arises out of different impulses and is directed toward
different ends than those behind much of the novel. The "grateful
memory" is not of scenes that were actually witnessed, but of those
that should have been witnessed, and this memory then leads to
predictable consequences. The pen is laid down, Thackeray the artist, the creator of *Vanity Fair,* ceases writing and travels into a realm
of poised and suspended beauty. The images captured not only embody that realm we saw more than six hundred pages earlier in
Dobbin's reverie but stand poignantly against that world through
which Thackeray has traveled in order to arrive at the cavern once
again. And in exploring this cavern, we hear not loud laughter and
boisterous gaiety but the interstices of silence, Mozart's music, and
the sounds of cows lowing as they troop down toward "long blue
shadows stretching over the grass."

But Thackeray must, of course, pick up his pen and become the creator of *Vanity Fair* once again; if art arises in part out of man's attempt to diminish the disparity between his dream and that world wherein his dreams may be either realized or frustrated, the artist must also listen to Wordsworth's "still, sad music of humanity" if he is to remind us of our own forgotten dreams. Thus the landscape disappears, but only to return again, perhaps in a different guise, yet nevertheless fulfilling similar needs and desires. And if Dobbin, Lady Steyne, and Thackeray cannot retain such an image or vision, they at least are allowed access to it; Becky Sharp, on the other hand, is denied such an experience, and it is primarily this lack of a remembered or re-created childhood that distinguishes her from the others—"but she had never been a girl, she said; she had been a woman since she was eight years old" (chap. 2), having forgotten "the time when she ever was young" (chap. 41). If there is an experience in Becky's life similar to such moments of recollection or reverie, it is in her attraction to the Bohemian life: "Becky liked the [Bohemian] life. She was at home with everybody in the place, pedlars, punters, tumblers, students and all. She was of a wild, roving nature, inherited from father and mother, who were both Bohemians, by taste and circumstance" (chap. 65). Such a life embodies, as image, a rebellion against the society in which she so earnestly wishes to succeed and also a spontaneity and inherent anarchy frequently associated by both Dickens and Thackeray with the life of the child or the life of the artist. The Bohemian life may not approximate childhood experience in its innocence or naïveté, but it is analogous to it insofar as it represents an outlawed state on the fringe of that civilized society Thackeray sees as a wilderness.

But when the novel ends, Becky is not in an artist's garret, but in a Ladies Society's charity booth and although she has premonitions of the deadening futility of the life she has chosen, "Becky loved society" and virtually all of her actions and values reaffirm rather than reject that civilization of which she is both symbol and victim. The charity booth Becky occupies at the novel's conclusion is both an enclave of piety and virtue amidst the world of Vanity Fair and an ironic, almost grotesque parody of the garden world that beckons Dobbin, Lady Steyne, and Thackeray himself. Within a booth representing neither compassion nor charity, but only the pretense of both, Becky as "reformed sinner," the benefactress of "hapless beings" from within her stalls "at Fancy Fairs," plays her inevitable last role; and it is finally, a role: seeing Dobbin and Amelia approach her in the stall, "she cast down her eyes demurely and smiled as they started away from her" (chap. 67).

IV

What judgment can finally be made of a novel that presents us with the darkened landscape of a nightmare and then, to allay the anxieties raised by such a landscape, offers us only the dream vision of a transitory and ethereal world? Thackeray's attempt to provide alternatives to the society he has delineated must be recognized, I think, as a qualified failure. But it is a failure born out of struggle rather than weakness, and out of artistic honesty rather than deception. Creating a work only partially understood and therefore frightening, Thackeray found it necessary to struggle free of the past while frequently possessing only the past's vocabulary and conceptual structures within which to define his freedom.

The kind of creative problems that this struggle produced is evidenced in Thackeray's attempt to place Dobbin at the center of the novel's moral vision. Having created a world which could no longer accommodate Rawdon Crawley, Thackeray removes him and is consequently left with Dobbin as the central male figure and does not, it seems, know quite what to do with him. Part of his dilemma is, if not allayed, at least postponed by absenting Dobbin from much of the novel's action after the Brussels episode; but when Dobbin returns to England, the problems he poses for Thackeray still exist. And in trying to cope with them, Thackeray returns to an image that the novel has already denied—namely, to the metaphor of the looking glass equitably reflecting the world around it. For example, late in the novel we are told that Dobbin is one of those "men whose aims are generous, whose truth is constant, and not only constant in its kind, but elevated in its degree; whose want of meanness makes them simple: who can look the world honestly in the face with an equal manly sympathy for the great and the small" (chap. 62). This is an admirable portrait of Dobbin; indeed, one suspects that it is too admirable, that Thackeray is straining too hard to convince us. And when the passage is examined, its idealizations are found to consist of clichés and a deadened vocabulary. Thackeray is describing an abstraction rather than a man and when we put flesh and blood on his ideal, the whole passage begins to sag. Given the world that Thackeray has by this point depicted, for one to look the world "honestly in the face" is to see what Rawdon saw and Thackeray himself sees. Similar efforts by Thackeray to bestow heroism upon Dobbin through inherited action sequences—for example, the rousing welcomes and the tearful send-offs that Dobbin receives during his trip through England—are equally ineffectual, although they do suggest the hold that previous definitions of heroism had on Thackeray's imagination. Such descriptions are borrowed from earlier concepts of the ideal gentleman, and however much we have to respect the impulses that sent Thackeray back to such concepts, they do not work within *Vanity Fair*.

The Dobbin we see in the novel's closing pages—aged, disheartened, and possessing a wisdom that does not lead to happiness—is a more credible and admirable figure. No longer cloaked with the rhetoric of heroism, Dobbin becomes a figure with whom Thackeray proceeds to the redefined nineteenth-century heroism we find, for example, in Dickens's Pip and Hardy's Jude. Thackeray moves in the conclusion of *Vanity Fair* toward a version of the pastoral, albeit equivocal, strained, and filled with internal tensions, with Dobbin as the shepherd of a small flock within Vanity Fair, providing it with his strength, protection, and love. But the world through which he moves has not changed; and when we speculate on the life awaiting his young daughter, we see her growing up within the same destructive society. Neither the active, if frustrated, heroism of a Rawdon Crawley nor the passive heroism of a William Dobbin is able to radiate outward and transform that world through which it moves. Thackeray has denied the political structure, the rural life, the isolated island, and, until the very end at least, the family as enduring sources of a value that can withstand the onslaught of Vanity Fair.

It has been observed before of the mid-nineteenth-century British novel that in it we begin to see evidence of a split or division between those impulses within the novel that move toward social realism and public myths of fulfillment on one hand and toward the modes of romance and private myths, dreams, and desires on the other. It is possible that the polarization we see in *Vanity Fair* as it evolves is further evidence of such a dissociation; and indeed it was one of Thackeray's more famous contemporaries, Charlotte Brontë, who seemed to intuit the nature of those tensions and radical undertones that arise as a consequence. In speaking of Thackeray in her preface to *Jane Eyre,* in its own right a potentially radical novel,

Brontë implicitly defines these two major and irreconciled impulses within *Vanity Fair*:

> I see in him an intellect profounder and more unique than his contemporaries have yet recognised; I regard him as the first social regenerator of the day—as the very master of that working corps who would restore to rectitude the warped system of things; . . . I think no commentator on his writings has yet found the comparison that suits him, the terms which rightly characterise his talent.

And earlier within the same preface, she also refers to Thackeray as "a man in our own days whose words are not framed to tickle delicate ears: who, to my thinking, comes before the great ones of society, much as the son of Imlah came before the throned Kings of Judah and Israel; and who speaks truth as deep, with a power as prophet-like and as vital."

Vanity Fair's power arises in large part from Thackeray's struggle to resolve the tension between those two impulses Brontë discerned in the novel—between that of the social satirist and critic and that of the visionary prophet. Thackeray was certainly not a political radical; indeed, like many of his contemporaries, he feared the populace or "mob" and was not about to suggest the overthrow of a known and tried system. More important, however, even if he had wanted to, it is unlikely that Thackeray could have provided us with alternatives from within any given political or social structure. He had earlier pointed out the facile solutions frequently offered by proletarian or industrial novels:

> There somehow arrives a misty reconciliation between the poor and the rich; a prophecy is uttered of better times for the one, and better manners in the other; presages are made of happy life, happy marriage and children, happy beef and pudding for all time to come; and the characters make their bow, grinning, in a group.
>
> (*Morning Chronicle*)

Within the solid tradition of English empirical meliorism, Thackeray understood that the road of social improvement was indeed a rough one, uneven, broken, at times retrogressive, and that the attempts of the novelist to pave that road were frequently embarrassing and ineffectual:

> A Trollope and a Disraeli, persons of fiery and poetical imagination, have gone astray when treading the crabbed labyrinths of political controversy; and not only gone astray, but, as it were, tripped, stumbled, broken their noses, and scratched themselves in an entirely ludicrous and undignified manner.
>
> (*Morning Chronicle*)

But Thackeray is also, as Brontë suggests, within the tradition of the artist as visionary, a tradition stretching behind him to Blake, Wordsworth, and Shelley, and before him to Morris, Hardy, and D. H. Lawrence. In one sense, this tradition is apolitical, but it also embraces the deepest meanings of politics. The redemption, however, which will bring forth the community these men envision, must, as Thackeray intuits, occur on a personal level, one apart from the changes that politics or economics can effect. Reaching in *Vanity Fair* toward an image that will inform with meaning and life the wilderness that is civilization, Thackeray finds such an image in the garden, which contains the forgotten childhood of his world and its inhabitants. As image, it is not original; but Thackeray's struggle in achieving and redefining it certainly earns him the right to call it his own.

This image haunts *Vanity Fair* and its creator, and like that background in the title-page illustration, it is apart from, yet very much within, the final landscape presented to us. And while it does not possess either the clarity of vision or the power that informs, for example, the later circuses of Dickens or the dances of Hardy, it is, I think, nevertheless, an image that arises out of similar impulses and responds to similar needs. At the end of *Vanity Fair*, it still stands—as it must—apart, isolated and inaccessible, except for brief moments of reverie. But if it is too remote to be permanently lived in, it is at the same time incapable of being permanently destroyed. Thus this image does endure, assuming different shapes, but continuing to haunt and to beckon those artists who travel through that world Thackeray saw so clearly in search of those values he could but tentatively express.

The Triumph of Clytemnestra: The Charades in *Vanity Fair*

Maria DiBattista

When Thackeray remarked that "the unwritten part of books . . . would be the most interesting," he meant, among other things, that the art of implication is the most subtle of authorial decorums. At no time in *Vanity Fair* is that art practiced so well as when Thackeray retires from the stage as "Manager" of his comic history and allows Becky Sharp to enact the tragic charade "The Triumph of Clytemnestra." It is a singular performance, played "with such ghastly truth" that it leaves the spectators speechless with fright and admiration. The scandalous identification of Becky, the novel's mock-heroic adventuress, with the heroic figure of the most majestic female dissembler in the chronicles of myth and history marks the culmination of Becky's career in the world of vanity. Implied in her "comic" rise from articled pupil to lady of fashion is the terrible project of Clytemnestra to revenge herself against a power both envied and resented.

The silent truth of Becky's "character" is reemphasized in her second major appearance as Clytemnestra. Her reassumption of Clytemnestra's demonic identity in the novel's penultimate illustration haunts the reader's imagination by ominously suggesting an ongoing campaign of vengeance, an undiminished talent for subterfuge, and, of course, the ghastly literalization of what in Becky's moment of triumph was represented as an "innocent" charade. In a murderous pantomime, a terrorized Jos Sedley pleads with the "Good

From *PMLA* 95, no. 5 (October 1980). © 1980 by the Modern Language Association of America.

Samaritan," Colonel Dobbin, to deliver him from the demonic schemer, while an inspired Becky balefully looks on from behind a curtain, seemingly awaiting the propitious moment to strike. The illustration presents an "interesting" (in Thackeray's sense) explanation of Sedley's suspicious death, for there is, in fact, no corresponding evidence in the written text to corroborate the visual testimony against Becky. The details of the illustration—and they are designedly indistinct—alone prove incriminating. Becky is Clytemnestra primarily in her *attitude,* in the aggressive and threatening stance she assumes toward her potential victim. Her hand, the agent of her murderous intention, is blurred in shadow, allowing just the suggestion of a poised weapon. The caption identifies Becky with Clytemnestra; the illustration insists on dark equivocations, on a shady and shadowy reality. The only verdict that can be rendered is Rawdon's anguished but legally dubious earlier judgment on Becky's seemingly treacherous conduct: "If she's not guilty, . . . she's as bad as guilty."

Thackeray claimed that behind all his personifications "there lies a dark moral, I hope" (*Papers*). But the meditative Thackerayan "I" who at times almost abuses his authorial license to intrude on the narrative with moral commentary remains conspicuously silent on the psychological, ethical, and social significance of Becky's impersonation of Clytemnestra and on the "dark moral" explicated through feminine retaliatory or "opportunistic" violence. He communicates Becky's affinity to Clytemnestra exclusively through the media of charade and illustration. In her two appearances as the murderous queen, Becky becomes pure icon, an unspeakable and speechless image of demonic womanhood. The garrulous narrator's uncharacteristic reticence in the presence of this icon has never been adequately remarked, much less explained. Thackeray refuses to make the obvious connection between Clytemnestra's rebellion against the warrior culture that authorizes the sacrifice of her child, Iphigenia, and his own extensive critique of the attitudes toward women and children in the bourgeois, jingoistic, mercantile culture of nineteenth-century England. He never interprets the material of the charade and illustration as a didactic allegory of the multiple vanities of familial, social, and political ambitions. Nor does he elaborate the myth of Clytemnestra into a cautionary tale or homiletic parable. He merely displaces it into a network of images that compose, in Dorothy Van Ghent's words, "the face of a gorgon of destiny."

Van Ghent skillfully traces the cultural derangements adumbrated in the novel's theme of "the fathers" to a classical and Freudian intuition of "the monstrous nature of man." Selecting for comment the "incidental" image of the chronometer "surmounted by a cheerful brass group of the sacrifice of Iphigenia" that summons the Osborne clan to its evening ritual meal, she remarks:

> The depths which are suggested by this picture, but quite as if accidentally, are the depths of Greek tragedy and, still further back, of Freud's dim, subhuman, imagined "primitive horde": the "dark leader" with his "hushed female company," and the ridiculous but furious Victorian clock "cheerfully" symbolizing the whole.

I would not argue with Van Ghent's view of Becky Sharp as the condensation of the "imperatively aggressive" and "insanely euphoric" attitudes prevailing in the morally sick civilization represented in *Vanity Fair*. I would only expand consideration of Thackeray's appropriation of classical material to interpret this pervasive cultural pathology. This essay first considers the charades that dramatize the dark classical moral represented in Thackeray's historical fabling and then examines his motive for innuendo, his reasons for submerging his classical and Freudian intuitions of cultural pathology in the depths of his picture of Vanity Fair.

II

It is part of the controlling conceit of Thackeray's novel to present history as an extended sequence of performances ("puppet shows") enacting a moral so dark that to illuminate it fully might be politically or spiritually perilous. Thackeray literalizes his controlling metaphor in the chapter "in which a charade is acted which may or may not puzzle the reader." But the apparent decision to clarify his metaphor is cunningly compromised by the riddling nature of the charades.

As a form of verbal "play," charades are designedly opaque. They attempt to communicate a hidden meaning, usually symbolized by a single word that assumes fetishistic properties because its meaning and form are shrouded in an often guilty secrecy. In charades the word is divided into its constituent sounds—the words within the word—and each component is dramatized. The audience, reader, or spectator must then recombine these "floating signifiers" to discover the whole word, whose original and primary significance is again dramatized at the end of the charade in the tableau of the Whole. Although charades appear to play freely with meaning, their "real" meaning is predetermined in a word that cannot be replaced by, or mistaken for, another word. In the best charades, those combining verbal wit with social or emotional "fact," the secret word representing the Whole denominates not only a sum greater than its constituent parts but the exact reverse of those parts. Such a feat of verbal reversal and transformation is illustrated in Jane Austen's *Emma* by Mr. Elton's charade for "courtship" or in Charlotte Brontë's *Jane Eyre* by the charades for "Bridewell," puzzled out by Rochester's fashionable guests. Brontë's charades, like Thackeray's, are particularly cunning in communicating their ghastly truth. As ironic wordplays, the charades reveal the private and unsuspected torment of Rochester and his mad, imprisoned wife, Bertha Mason, through publicly enacting the word's two syllables, in tableaux that seem especially grim given the innocent surfaces of "Bride" and "well."

Charades, then, are never totally gratuitous forms of entertainment. They constitute a mode of verbal double-dealing that involves and often implicates the actors or spectators—sometimes both—in the social or psychological reality dramatized. Charades are dumb shows "to catch the conscience of the king" by playing out a deliberately concealed evil, an ignored social danger, or an obscure external menace or private horror. The incriminating potential of charades is emphasized by the disguises and roles adopted by the concealing-revealing performers who enact them. Thus Thackeray identifies the characters in the first series of charades—Colonel Crawley as Agamemnon, Becky as Clytemnestra—but their social identity dissolves, although not completely, into the drama they enact without being technically guilty. Characters thus assume roles in a play whose meaning is made transparent *through* them but is not necessarily made transparent *to* them. Their assigned roles are charged with a characteristic Thackerayan innuendo and equivocation; to repeat the judgment of Colonel Crawley, these performers, if not guilty, are as bad as guilty. And the same may be said of those in complicity with them—the audience of the charades.

It is the emotionally felt presumption of personal or cultural guilt that pervades and shadows the apparently "innocent" entertainments at *Vanity Fair*'s Gaunt House. The charades begin with an oriental tableau depicting a Turkish dignitary and voluptuary examining the "wares" of an Eastern slave trade. Despite the exotic decor evoking an alien, barbaric milieu, the initial moments of this charade announce a universal, not a historically localized, cultural pathology: sexual bondage, enslavement, exploitation, and victimization. As a Nubian slave makes his obeisant salaams to "my lord the Aga," the fashionable audience responds with a "thrill of terror and delight," a spontaneous demonstration of feeling that betrays an "exquisite" and volatile sexual fantasy of demonic virility that lies perilously close to the surface of the audience's "civilized" consciousness.

The icons of sexual imperialism that abound in this charade implicate the spectator-audience in the guilt, not of association, but of attitude, as Becky's second appearance as Clytemnestra suggests. Thus the Nubian slave's obeisant salaams to the Kislar Aga eerily recall and comment on the attitude of the idolatrous and slavish Amelia, who, on her wedding night, prostrates herself before her master, George Osborne. And the audience's "thrill of terror and delight" echoes George's own exquisite sensation as he gazes on the "slave before him in that simple yielding faithful creature" and feels his soul thrill within him, the "Sultan's thrill" in sexual mastery and "the knowledge of his complete power." In exposing the secret fantasies of sexual appropriation masquerading as "lawful matrimonial pleasures," Thackeray attempts his subtlest, perhaps most damaging penetration into the dark and tumultuous instincts underlying the civilized structures of sexual conduct and the social institution of marriage.

The aestheticizing of these sadomasochistic yearnings is represented in the ensuing sequence of the tableau when the entreaties of the beautiful slave girl asking to be returned to her Circassian lover are contemplated as composing an attitude of "beautiful despair." The "obdurate Hassan" only laughs at her sentimental notion of the Circassian bridegroom, mocking the slave girl's "Arcadian Simplicity" in believing that love, not power, determines the destiny of women in the markets of Vanity Fair. The tableau, which contrasts the "genteel" fictions of disinterested love with the sexual imperialism of a rich and decadent culture, is resolved through a sudden and completely illusory deus ex machina. The repressed takes its revenge on the oppressor, as the Kislar Aga, the black eunuch of the oriental harem, brings in a letter, a ghastly joy transfiguring his face. In an ecstasy of revenge, "grinning horribly," and ignoring the Pasha's cry for mercy, the Kislar Aga pulls out a bowstring. The denouement of this revenger's tragedy is eclipsed in a sudden and decorous blackout that hides the "dark deed" from public view.

The orientalism of this charade may shield the audience from the dramatic immediacy of the eunuch's murderous revenge. Yet it also provides more than a distancing backdrop against which all contagious fantasies can be played out without fear of censure. The oriental setting accumulates into itself all Thackeray's previous suggestions in the novel that beneath England's treatment of women—hypostasized in the Victorian cult of angelic womanhood—abides an uregenerate barbarity, a "Turkish" lust for mastery: "We are Turks with the affections of our women," the narrator had earlier remarked of the "poor little martyr" Amelia, "and have made them subscribe to our doctrine too." Through Amelia, the angelic figure of self-sacrificing, self-effacing womanhood whose "gentle little heart" obeys "not unwillingly" such despotic doctrines, Thackeray is forced to examine the psychology of female martyrdom. The slave girl in the charades is only a public symbol of Amelia's private enslavement to a whole system of cultural imperatives. When the narrator attempts to "peer into those dark places where the torture is administered" to such willing victims, he sees a sight so pitiable and incriminating that he breaks out into a hysterical apostrophe to subjugated women that combines compassion for their plight with relief at his own masculine exemption from their "long and ignoble bondage":

> O you poor women! O you poor secret martyrs and victims, whose life is a torture, who are stretched on racks in your bedrooms, and who lay your heads down on the block daily at the drawing-room table; every man who watches your pains, or peers into those dark places where the torture is administered to you, must pity you—and—and thank God that he has a beard.

It is clear that Thackeray harbors no *intrinsic* respect for "the romance and the sentiment of sacrifice" as an expressive vehicle of heroic womanhood, for it is precisely such idealizations that secure Amelia's bondage. The narrator's voyeuristic penetration into the dark chambers of the feminine psyche that house such sentiments unmans him, and he retreats, in a kind of willing "blackout" of his aroused consciousness, from the pitiable spectacle by recalling, uneasily and rather comically, the sexual symbol of his difference and his exemption from such torture—his beard. Such unnerving glimpses of secret martyrdom, unwitnessed victimization, and "Gothic" savagery are appropriated by the first component of the charade word—"Aga," a cultural symbol of sexual barbarity infecting private life and expanded into public and political forms.

The second charade retains the Eastern background, but the suggestion of violence has been suppressed and transformed into a peaceful tableau. The eunuch has resigned himself to impotent passivity, and Zuleika, the despairing pastoral lover, is now perfectly reconciled to her victimizer, the Hassan. There is hardly any action in the scene. Instead, interest centers on the imposing figure of an enormous Egyptian head, from which issues a comic song composed by Mr. Wagg. The dominating figure alludes to the Ethiopian king Memnon. Acording to Lemprière's *Bibliotheca Classica,* Thackeray's favorite source for classical material, Memnon's heroic death was commemorated by an enormous statue that possessed "the wonderful property of uttering a melodious sound every day, at sun-rising, like that which is heard at the breaking of the string of a harp when it is wound up." The statue and the legend it symbolizes emphasize the metamorphic properties of violence. Memnon was killed in combat with Achilles in defense of Priam's Troy. His mother, Aurora, was so disconsolate at the death of her son that she pleaded with Zeus to grant her sacrificed child an honor that might immortalize him. Zeus complied, and from the funeral pyre of Memnon there arose a flight of birds, the Memnonides. The myth is composed of several motifs involving scenes of violent, yet ultimately stabilizing metamorphosis: the metamorphosis of Memnon's bloody death into the seasonal return of the Memnonides in ritual commemoration of the Ethiopian monarch; the transformation of violence into an artifact of civilization; the translation of grief into art, suffering into song. It is this final transformation that is emphasized in the "singing head" of the charade.

The peaceful harmony of this tableau vivant soon proves illusory, however, as the pacific and comic song issuing from the death's-head modulates into the unexpectedly dissonant and sublime chords of "the awful music of Don Juan." Like Agamemnon, Don Juan represents a type of sexually imperial masculinity with an immoderate appetite for power, and the strains from the opera provide a rhetorically musical bridge connecting the archaic bloodlusts of a barbaric civilization (the "subject" of the charades) with the sexual vendettas disrupting a more contemporary aristocratic milieu (the social "subject" of *Vanity Fair*). In the Mozartian opera of seduction and betrayal, of sexual transgression and retribution in the name of family honor or divine vengeance, Thackeray sees the same cultural ethos working out its evil destiny: a corrupt ideology of sexual imperialism underlying the myth of love in the Western world. The last of Thackeray's historical charades reveals the secret identity and cultural primacy of his central figure of virility—Agamemnon, a curious compound of heroic and barbaric manhood: an "Aga," a figure of sexual barbarism; a "Memnon," a figure of cultural authority and prestige. With mordant irony, Thackeray bestows on Agamemnon the epithet *anax andron,* the kingly man who will soon pay for the excesses of his manhood and of his kingship. In a sweeping and majestic gesture of feminine revenge, Clytemnestra, alias Becky Crawley, steals the dagger from the hesitant Aegisthus to complete the retribution, but here again the outcome is overcome by darkness.

The scene of the second series of charades moves to more familiar territory, as if to escape the malignancy and potency of the oriental and classical material dramatized in the first sequence. Thackeray's setting is now Fieldingesque, evoking the atmosphere of low-life farce and the memory of an earlier England where evil took the benign form of rascality. The first tableau of the second series depicts a comic "night" scene in a country house. The action is desultory: two bagmen play a game of cribbage, a chambermaid warms up the beds and wards off the bagmen's advances. The scene ends to the dreamy cadences of "Dormez, dormez, chers Amours." If the virulent "Amantium Irae" is exposed and released in the Clytemnestra-Agamemnon charade, here the strain is transposed and modulated into sweeter amatory tones anticipating the love lyric, "The Rose upon My Balcony," that concludes the entertainments.

But the submerged motif of sexual horror reasserts itself in the second tableau of the new series. The scene remains the same, but the insignia of the house is now revealed to be the Steyne arms, the chivalric "coronets and carved heraldry" that Thackeray has already described as bearing "the dark mark of fate and doom." Thus even though the scene resembles the merry comings and goings of *Tom Jones*'s Upton Inn ("inn," of course, is the syllable dramatized in this tableau), the Steyne arms visually suggest an invisible, internal, and still potent fatality at work, recalling Thackeray's earlier hint that a sexual curse haunts the Steyne house:

> It was the mysterious taint of the blood: the poor mother had brought it from her own ancient race. The evil had broken out once or twice in the father's family, long before Lady Steyne's sins had begun, or her fasts and tears and penances had been offered in their expiation.

An Aeschylean brooding over the fall of the great house informs Thackeray's account of evil communicating itself through the mysterious "stain" or taint of blood brought from an ancient race, an ancestral evil that hangs over Gaunt House as a dark reminder of the time "when the pride of the race was struck down as the firstborn of Pharaoh." The original sin embodied in the fatal union of the Steynes becomes the focus of the deepest progenitive anxieties about familial succession, patrimony, and the decline and eclipse of the aristocracy as a historical heritage. The charades' suppressed Ovidian theme of metamorphosis and their Aeschylean vision of sexual fate and familial doom combine to revive the repressed but never forgotten memory of unexpiated and unexpiable sins that will be violently avenged. Ominous hints of an avenging agent and future retribution are conveyed in the final "rustle" of movement at the end of the "inn" charade. As the curtain is drawn, a mysterious, though eminent, guest is being announced, perhaps an Orestes bent on revenge or, as Thackeray intimates, a Ulysses preparing for another kind of bloody homecoming. Christian hopes in the efficacy of penance (the expiatory prayers of Lady Steyne) are eclipsed by the urgency and power of these classical foreshadowings of an inevitable historical reckoning. They are only revived, belatedly, in the mark of Cain that Lord Steyne, after his failed attempt to appease Rawdon and exculpate himself, bears as the "scar" inflicted by Colonel Crawley, the avenging returned husband, in the melodramatic scene that marks the catastrophe of Becky and Steyne's illicit liaison.

In the final syllable of the second series of charades, anxieties about an impending cultural crisis provoked by the domestic tragedies and hypocrisies of a decaying aristocracy are concentrated into an image of imperial (political) fear. The final tableau shows a ship foundering in unruly seas, despite the heartening medley of "Rule Britannia." The spectacle of the imperiled ship of state, conventional symbol of maritime England, speaks to the most frightening nightmare haunting the British political mind. As the music of the tableau "rises up to the wildest pitch of stormy excitement," discharging itself in "gale," the source of the audience's uneasy, turbulent emotion (the specter of political unrest and unrule) is mollified by the transfiguration of Becky into Philomele. The charade completes its word: Philomele, "the night-in-gale."

The pairing of Clytemnestra and Philomele in the character of Becky Sharp is neither fortuitous nor incongruous. Philomele's story, like Clytemnestra's, constitutes an elaborate narration of sexual deception, brutality, violation of sacred familial bonds, and violent reprisal. Philomele is also a figure of outraged womanhood, literally concealed and silenced by her sexual seducer and tormentor, Tereus, king of Thrace, husband to Philomele's sister, Procne. Tereus's crimes against Philomele, whom he imprisons and mutilates by cutting out her tongue, are, like Agamemnon's, doubly grave, being the sins of both king and husband. Philomele, deprived of a voice to protest her ravishment, communicates the chronicle of her sufferings through art—the tapestry she weaves to tell of the sins of the fathers, the living fabric of primal wrongs. Like the scenes that evoke her presence, Philomele's speechless art reenacts the hidden outrage and silently protests against the oppressor's power. It is Procne who reads the tale and, like Clytemnestra, disguises her resentments while plotting her treacherous revenge. During the Bacchic orgies she murders her son Itys and serves him to the brutal and brutalizing Tereus in a grisly feast. When Tereus learns of this cannibalistic and retributive rite, his rage is predictably extreme, but his murderous designs against Philomele and Procne are forestalled by his own transformation into a hoopoe, Philomele's into a nightingale, Procne's into a swallow, and Itys's into a pheasant.

These grim classical legends of metamorphosis, fatal sexual unions, incestuous intrigue, familial cannibalism, sacrificed children, and female retaliation mirror and complement Agamemnon and Clytemnestra's family tragedy and, of course, all the incestuous, spiritually cannibalizing relationships in *Vanity Fair*. Thackeray seems to be following the late, Ovidian version of the myth that makes Philomele the nightingale and Procne the swallow, perhaps because the Ovidian reinterpretation attributes both pathos and the power of representation to the mute, raped sister rather than to the betrayed and betraying wife. The Ovidian version allows Thackeray to suggest the essential doubleness of Becky as a figure of cultural evil, representing a Clytemnestra and a Philomele, the ravisher and the ravished, the unscrupulous avenger and the plaintive victim. Thackeray's double image of female fatality culminates in the much remarked description of Becky as a siren of magical powers who lures men to their watery graves. (Clytemnestra simply lures Agamemnon to his bath to kill him.) The Becky-siren, "singing and smiling, coaxing and cajoling," conceals from view a "monster's hideous tail, . . . writhing and twirling, diabolically hideous and slimy." The snake-siren image reveals more about the narrator's erotic imagination than it does about Becky's fatal sexuality, betraying as it does the sexual disgust and fear lurking beneath the "perfectly genteel and inoffensive manner" in which he relates her fiendish (Bohemian) adventures. If Becky is a monster with a remarkable and growing "taste for disrespectability," she is no *lusus naturae*, no freak of nature, but a freak of the culture whose model of angelic womanhood elevates the religious over the erotic instinct. Becky's "disreputable" character represents the potential for a demonic and malevolent female sexuality in contrast to the respectable but no less selfish "love" of her true opposite and double, Amelia, the martyr to the Victorian feminine ideal who dedicates her life to the "corpse" of her love.

III

It was George Eliot who reminded us, citing the authority of Herodotus, that the woman question is not an extraneous or a peripheral factor in the historical analysis of change but a "fit beginning." Like Eliot's *Middlemarch, Vanity Fair* centers on the lot of women in its description of the origins of cultural crisis and its prophetic assessments of the possibilities for meaningful change. When Thackeray decides to forgo a military history celebrating England's heroic manhood during the Napoleonic era for a comic history chronicling the amatory and financial fortunes of female "non–combatants" and the men who love them, his decision is neither historically frivolous nor inconsequential. The stories of Becky Sharp and Amelia Sedley expand into paradigmatic fables paralleling and reflecting "those mutations which ages produce in empires, cities, and boroughs," mutations that are recorded in the migration of power from the landed gentry to an ascendant middle class with a ready-money, credit economy.

In the declining aristocracy (whose historical eclipse Thackeray dramatizes by the deep degeneracy of Sir Pitt Crawley presiding over the "rotten borough" of Queen's Crawley, by the cynicism of Lord Steyne, and by the "Dowagerism" reigning in Great Gaunt Street and in the rising merchant classes (which he treats satirically), Thackeray perceives, but cannot totally disavow, the same corrupt and corrupting sexual ideology, the wholesale "selling" and emotional victimization of women to ensure the traditional primacy and the economic power of an imperiled social caste. Marriage thus becomes the instrument of social and political ambitions, and all sexual attitudes serve to rationalize even as they dissimulate this fundamental, sexually "politic" economy.

Thackeray's formal appropriation of the Clytemnestra myth in the novel serves as a psychological and *historical* commentary on the unexamined delusions of the Victorians' sexual ideology. To identify Becky as Clytemnestra is not merely to invoke a psychological explanation for Becky's "natural" wickedness but to suggest that in the conduct of life the public and the private, the national and the domestic remain inseparable. Attitudes toward women, marriage, sex, because they are present at the very formation and foundation of a cultural order, constitute the primary basis of cultural and social stability. Ideology is all of a piece, so that the private tyrannies authorized by familial self-interest do not confine themselves to the domestic sphere but invariably and inevitably radiate to infect a society's conception of itself and to motivate the most decisive of national actions.

Becky Sharp is a representative figure whose social ambitions reflect the internal crisis of oppressed womanhood and the external menace of a "French" radicalism comically treated in the "bel esprit" of Miss Crawley, who passionately embraces Voltaire and Rousseau and talks "most energetically of the rights of women." Becky's radicalism is more subversive and disarming. Her mother was a Frenchwoman, and Becky's morals seem indebted to the darker elements in French novels. In the denigration and humiliation of women, Thackeray discerns a universal principle of violation that provides the logic of his domestic comedy and informs his intuition, pristinely classical in its pessimism, of the cycle of reprisal that underlies and determines all historical events. In one of the novel's few sustained moments of seriousness, the narrator comments on the historically decisive battle of Waterloo, a comment that is hauntingly applicable to the outrages committed and authorized by the bitter necessities of war for which Clytemnestra courts revenge in the *Agamemnon:*

> You and I, who were children when the great battle was won and lost, are never tired of hearing and recounting the history of that famous action. Its remembrance rankles still in the bosoms of millions of countrymen of those brave men who lost the day. They pant for an opportunity of revenging that humiliation; and if a contest, ending in a victory on their part, should ensue, elating them in their turn, and leaving its cursed legacy of hatred and rage behind to us, there is no end to the so-called glory and shame, and to the alternations of successful and unsuccessful murder, in which two high-spirited nations might engage. Centuries hence, we Frenchmen and Englishmen might be boasting and killing each other still, carrying out bravely the Devil's Code of honour.

Shame and glory are the values endemic to a classical ethos, and their legacy is a cursed heritage of hatred and rage, the alternations of successful and unsuccessful murder. In contemplating the sweeping panorama of historical change and struggle, Thackeray discerns an endlessly repeatable cycle of victimization and revenge. Nor is this legacy confined to intercultural, international conflict. The organizing conceit of his novel centers on the interpenetrating metaphors of military and amatory campaigns to secure "positions," establish power, defend hegemony. And the deep interdependence, even identity, between acts of love and war, caricatured in the illustration depicting the comic *mésalliance* of Venus preparing the armor of Mars, penetrates far into the rhetoric of the novel's social and political satire. Through the controlling image of embattled relations, Thackeray suggests that tyrannies and servilities corrupting the foundation of social life eventually infect the entire cultural order. The mutually reinforcing projects of sexual and political revenge are symbolized in the Iphigenia chronometer, whose steady and remorseless ticking signals an ongoing, if unsuspected, cycle of aggression and retaliation. Becky's second appearance as Clytemnestra keeps this classical concept of familial, racial, and national fatality alive. It suggests that the "strife" between men and women, between the outraged female and the kingly male, is a strife not confined to private realms but, as Clytemnestra warns the chorus in the *Agamemnon,* a "conflict born out of ancient bitterness . . . pondered deep in time."

Thackeray's classicism in *Vanity Fair,* then, validates rather than contradicts the novel's critical realism and its narrative objective: "to expose," as Lukács rightly argues, "contemporary apologetics" (*The Historical Novel*). The mythological material that supports the novel's cultural interpretation and social criticism both reflects and anticipates the resurgent "paganism" whose "dark morals" will dominate the historical imagination of the second half of the nineteenth century. In this sense, *Vanity Fair* is an intriguing transitional text between the self-confident neoclassical novels of Fielding, who could develop potentially contagious Oedipal material within a transforming Christian vision of providentially ordered history, and the bitter, darkly pagan Aeschylean tragedies of Thomas Hardy. As the last two major illustrations of *Vanity Fair* testify, depicting the double face of Becky Sharp as Clytemnestra and as an ironic exemplum of "Virtue Rewarded," there exists an uneasy and problematic alliance between Thackeray's classical intuitions of cultural disorder and the Christian vision implied by his novel's ironic appropriation of its allegorical original, *Pilgrim's Progress.* The charades, the "play" within the larger historical performance enacted in the novel, are representative of Thackeray's dilemma and his proposed solution: through their *formal* opacity and equivocation, they suggest that the meaning of historical act or cultural "attitude" must be supplied, puzzled out by the spectator or reader. Thackeray deliberately displaces meaning into the external and alienating realm of impersonation, symbolic identification, and illustration, where it is subject to multiple, often faulty interpretations, even though, as the charades tell us, only one conclusion is right and inevitable.

The generic imperative of the charades is never to expose reality in the direct light of complete representation. It is this imperative that shadows and perhaps explains Thackeray's reluctance as a narrator to interpret the central classical myths of the novel and to expose Becky as guilty or innocent of certain sexual or social crimes. Thackeray's reticence in dealing explicitly with these issues may have something to do with the moral climate of his time, but his carefully chosen moments of silence originate, I would suggest, in a kind of ritual reluctance and fear at unveiling the deeper mysteries or hidden laws governing the fate of any society. Vanity, for Thackeray as for the Preacher, is the false idol of the unregenerate historical world, its dark divinity incarnated in the "Imperial Master," the "Magnificent Idea," the "August Presence" of the king who rules. As Thackeray prepares to initiate his readers into what he had earlier called the "mystical language" of vanity and to usher them into the very penetralia of mystery—the entertainments that provide the "high world" of fashion and power with its social rituals—he tellingly invokes the tutelary myth of Semele:

> They say the honest newspaper-fellow who sits in the hall and takes down the names of the great ones who are admitted to the feasts, dies after a little time. He can't survive the glare of fashion long. It scorches him up, as the presence of Jupiter in full dress wasted that poor imprudent Semele—a giddy moth of a creature who ruined herself by venturing out of her natural atmosphere. Her myth ought to be taken to heart amongst the Tyburnians, the Belgravians,—her story, and perhaps Becky's too.

Thackeray's attempt to allegorize the story of Semele into a comic parable of social vanity and class "imprudence," like his Clytemnestra charade, is only partially successful in concealing the generative meaning of the myth. Semele, a mortal, gains knowledge of divine and immutable form at the expense of her life; her story, and Becky's too, constitutes a cautionary myth linking the *éclaircissement* of the knower with a destructive, if generative, violence that is essentially sexual. Thackeray's allusion to this myth of sexual violence and violation introduces a variation on the novelistic theme of unhappy unions, a theme previously limited to the comic treatment of *"mésalliance"*: the imprudent marriage of Amelia Sedley and George Osborne.

The myth of Semele establishes a correspondence between demystification and annihilation that is crucial in understanding Thackeray's own attitudes toward novelistic knowledge, especially narrative omniscience. Complete knowledge becomes at best an instrument of historical and personal devaluation, as when the narrator "enlightens" his readers that the relics sent to Miss Crawley to effect a reconciliation between Rawdon and his aunt were purchased from peddlers trafficking in the spoils of war. "The novelist," advises the narrator in sardonic tones, "who knows everything, knows this also." Here omniscience is in the service of Thackeray's "cynicism," but the narrator is merely laughing up the reader's sleeve. At worst, complete demystification constitutes what Ruskin, in his troubled response to *Vanity Fair,* calls "blasphemy"—in its scriptural sense of " 'Harmful Speaking'—not against God only, but against man, and against all the good works and purposes of Nature":

> The word is accurately opposed to "Euphemy," the right or well-speaking of God and His world; and the two modes of speech are those which, going out of the mouth, sanctify or defile the man.
>
> Going out of the mouth, that is to say, deliberately and of purpose. A French postillion's "Sacr-r-re"—loud, with the low "Nom de Dieu" following between his teeth, is not blasphemy, unless against his horse; but Mr. Thackeray's close of his Waterloo chapter in *Vanity Fair,* "And all night long Amelia was praying for George, who was lying on his face, dead, with a bullet through his heart" (sic), is blasphemy of the most fatal and subtle kind.

Ruskin's appropriation of the vocabulary of the sacred to interpret the "speech" of omniscient narration locates the source of sanctity or defilement in the speaker, not in the reality of the thing spoken. Thackeray's blasphemy in the Waterloo chapter is authorized, however, by the conventions of realism that prescribe the unbiased chronicling of event unmediated by palliative illusion. But in the charades of *Vanity Fair,* in the question of Becky's guilty liaison with Lord Steyne, and in the suspicious death of Jos Sedley, Thackeray resorts neither to voiced blasphemy nor to its Ruskinian opposite, euphemy. Rather he resorts to blasphemy's negation: an equivocal and equivocating silence. His *ultimate* reluctance to expose the illusion of love and the myth of good works emanating from God, man, and nature leads him to abscond, like a tormented demiurge, from the scene of the performances, leaving the stage of his history free for his performers to act out blasphemy without speaking it.

Perhaps it is the story of Semele ("her story, and . . . Becky's too") that remains the fable Thackeray takes most to heart. As the myth suggests, Thackeray's critical silences could betray an anxiety, religious or metaphysical, about the limits of the human power to know and to represent. It is an anxiety Thackeray covertly expresses in his life of Swift, where he sees in Swift's genius—a genius almost

Zeus-like in its power "to flash upon falsehood and scorch it into perdition"—an awful and an evil spirit. Thackeray describes Swift in a passage that recalls Semele's imprudent exposure to the glare of a dazzling magnificence:

> In his old age, looking at the "Tale of a Tub," when he said, "Good God, what a genius I had when I wrote that book!" I think he was admiring, not the genius, but the consequences to which the genius had brought him—a vast genius, a magnificent genius, a genius wonderfully bright, and dazzling, and strong,—to seize, to know, to see, to flash upon falsehood and scorch it into perdition, to penetrate into the hidden motives, and expose the black thoughts of men,—an awful, an evil spirit.

What Thackeray seems to fear in the example of Swift's life and the methods of his art is the fate ordained for the evil genius capable of penetrating into hidden motives and exposing the black thoughts of men: the "maddened hurricane" of a tormented man who suffered "frightfully from the consciousness of his own scepticism" and who "bent his pride so far down as to put his apostasy out to hire." The subjectivism underlying Thackeray's belief that Swift's art was inspired by the misanthropic resentments of a failed opportunist may reflect Thackeray's own fear of spiritual bankruptcy, a fear dramatized in the cynical apostasy of the haunted Lord Steyne, over whose head hovers the Damoclean sword of madness. It is this fear that may explain Thackeray's moral and ideological ambivalence in *Vanity Fair,* an ambivalence Arnold Kettle has defined as the desire to "expose illusions and yet keep them" (*An Introduction to the English Novel*). Such ambivalence lies at the heart of Thackeray's "gentlemanly ideal," an ideal that endorses the class-bound ideology his satire exposes.

Thackeray himself defends the moral status of silence when he defines Amelia's reticence as "the timid denial of the unwelcome assertion of ruling folks, a tacit protestantism." In Thackeray's tacit protestantism, so different from the vocal and charged denunciations of Swift, he lays to rest his social and narrative anxieties and exorcises the Swiftian specter of prophetic madness. It is such tacit protestantism that characterizes the melancholic anomie of the novel's broken or inconclusive ending: "Come children, let us shut up the box and the puppets, for our play is played out."

Having opened up a Pandora's box of social and historical evils, Thackeray vainly tries to shut them up in the confines of his fictional puppet box, to "miniaturize" and thus minimize the implications of his fable. As a satirist and critical realist, Thackeray is hopelessly divided between his evil genius for penetration into the hidden motives and invisible laws governing human relations and his Steyne-like cynicism in exposing a reality at once spiritually vain and morally horrifying. Charlotte Brontë rightly saw that the satirist of *Vanity Fair* could lift "the mask from the face of the Pharisee" through the "Greek fire of his sarcasm," but she mistakenly placed the "levin-brand of denunciation" in the tradition of biblical prophecy. If *Vanity Fair* often speaks as "solemn as an oracle," its testimony does not resemble the "faithful counsel" of a Micaiah prophesying evil ("Preface" to *Jane Eyre,* dedicated to Thackeray). When Thackeray speaks, he speaks like the impotent prophetess Cassandra, who, in chronicling the *Agamemnon's* dark drama of sexual vengeance, laments that "there is no god of healing in this story." (l. 1248)

The Comedy
of Shifting Perspectives

Robert M. Polhemus

> *In comedy, therefore, there is a general trivialization of the human battle.*
> SUSANNE K. LANGER

Vanity Fair makes a mockery of life in a capitalizing world. Thackeray's comic vision works to create perspectives that free consciousness from the vanities of a commercial and competitive society. Though this world may betray, hurt, and even kill us, it is, above all else, ridiculous; since we can see its follies and make fun of its ways, it need not enthrall our minds. Such, in brief, is the argument and the release that *Vanity Fair*'s comedy offers.

A novel of shifting, sometimes confusing, perspectives, it gives its readers just what it demands from them: a flexible and subtle way of seeing and judging the world. I want to get at Thackeray's comic vision through two crucial passages from *Vanity Fair*. The first is the famous ending of the novel: "Ah! *Vanitas Vanitatum!* Which of us is happy in this world? Which of us has his desire? or, having it, is satisfied?—Come children, let us shut up the box and the puppets, for our play is played out." That sums up the situation in "this world," i.e., the particular kind of world that he has just defined for us in hundreds of thousands of words. The conclusion implies possibilities of liberation from it, if we see it in proper perspective.

Words like "perspective" and "focus" come naturally in dis-

From *Comic Faith: The Great Tradition from Austen to Joyce.* © 1980 by the University of Chicago. University of Chicago Press, 1980.

cussing Thackeray. Optics, point of view, reflection, and composition fascinated this illustrator of his own books and would-be painter, as the second passage shows. Thackeray is describing a room in the Osborne's house: "The great glass over the mantle-piece, faced by the other great console glass at the opposite end of the room, increased and multiplied between them the brown Holland bag in which the chandelier hung; until you saw these brown Holland bags fading away in endless perspectives, and this apartment of Miss Osborne's seemed the centre of a system of drawing-rooms" (chap. 42). This paragraph serves nicely as a metaphor for the novel and its structure: reflections on reflections amid the mirroring vanities of man. Here we have changing frames of reference, important allusions in visions of trivia, and a whole social system revealed by glittering surfaces. In the reverberation and cross-tension of opposing views, we get the literal belittling of a society, expanded dimensions of meaning through optical analogy, and a converging of audience and scene in the narrative point of view. What comic expression is to Dickens, comic perspective is to Thackeray: the thing that makes life bearable.

REFLECTIONS

The world is a looking-glass.
Vanity Fair, chap. 2

Good God dont I see (in that may-be cracked and warped looking glass in which I am always looking) my own weaknesses wickednesses lusts follies short-comings?

Thackeray, *Letters*

Vanity Fair is the Versailles of novels; it features conspicuous looking-glasses, both metaphorical and real. Fittingly, the frontispiece shows a lounging performer in motley peering into a cracked speculum. A *mirror*—one of the meanings of the "vanity" of the title—is a miracle of artifice that allows us to go out of ourselves. Looking at it, one becomes both viewing subject and visualized object, both in and beyond what one sees. In its shiny surface, this tool of reflection multiplies eyes, selves, and perspectives.

For Thackeray, the complex process of reflection defines human life. Mind, world, and art are mirrors reflecting upon one another, and every reflection for him is a reflection both *of* and *on* something. That is why the Osborne glasses make such a perfect symbol for his art. When he reflected, he saw contradictions in himself and his world, and they take form in the mirroring polarities that give the novel its dialectical tension and emotional force: for example, Becky/ Amelia, cynicism/sentimentality, stasis/progress, resignation/rebellion, characters/audience. He organizes and develops in *Vanity Fair* reflections of and on his era, his self, and the myths, modes, and concerns of previous literature.

I

Specifically, a massive and conscious reflection on two major religious texts, the Book of Ecclesiastes and *The Pilgrim's Progress,* forms the basis of the novel. It mediates and secularizes through comedy the cosmic fatalism of the one and the apocalyptic fervor of the other. Like them, it offers the pleasures of condemning the world, but it also makes the world laughable. Thackeray insists on making explicit the growing tendency of comic fiction to reflect and perform the traditional functions of religious faith. He claimed for himself and other humorists the office of "week-day preacher": "our profession seems to me to be as serious as the Parson's own," he said of all "who set up as Satirical-Moralists." "One is bound to speak the truth as far as one knows it, whether one mounts a cap and bells or a shovel-hat; and a great deal of disagreeable matter must come out in the course of such an undertaking" (chap. 8). This apostle of humor as moral strategy, as that frontispiece shows, comes to us as Ecclesiastes in long-eared livery and John Bunyan transported through the Victorian looking-glass.

Thackeray's "Ah! *Vanitas Vanitatum*" recalls its source in Ecclesiastes, shedding light on his content and purpose:

> Vanity of vanities, saith the Preacher, . . . all is vanity.
> (Eccles. 1:2)

> I have seen all the works that are done under the sun; and behold, all is vanity and vexation of spirit.
> (Eccles. 1:14)

> Vanity of vanities, saith the preacher; all is vanity. And moreover, because the preacher was wise, he still taught the people knowledge; yea, he gave good heed, and sought out, and set in order many proverbs. The preacher sought

to find out acceptable words: and that which was written
was upright, even words of truth. The words of the wise
are as goads, and as nails fastened by the masters of as-
semblies.

(Eccles. 12:8–11)

"Yesterday's preacher," writes Thackeray in *The English Humorists*,
"becomes the text for today's sermon." The text is Ecclesiastes'
skeptical world-view, the sermon is *Vanity Fair*, and the comic
"week-day preacher" renders the meaning and form of *vanitas
vanitatum* for his time.

The title and concept of the novel, of course, come from the
Vanity Fair passage in *The Pilgrim's Progress from This World to That
Which Is to Come*. This original fair is first of all a place of buying and
selling, and Thackeray magnifies and develops every nuance and
implication in Bunyan's description: "at this fair are all such merchandise sold, as houses, lands, trades, places, honours, preferments,
titles, countries, kingdoms, lusts, pleasures, and delights of all sorts,
as whores, bawds, wives, husbands, children, masters, servants,
lives, blood, bodies, souls, silver, gold, pearls, precious stones, and
what not." He expands and makes specific for his century this allegorical vision of the world as one vast commerical enterprise. Every
item that Bunyan lists as merchandise is bought and sold in the
novel.

II

Vanity Fair is epic; it is the history of a culture—what Thackeray
calls his "little world of history" (chap. 1). But it is an epic that
mocks and mimics, the true comic epic in prose that Fielding had
called for a century before. The opening reflects Victorian civilization as surely as Achilles' shield reflects the heroic age, but it also has
an undertone of ridicule:

While the present century was in its teens, and on one
sunshiny morning in June, there drove up to the great iron
gate of Miss Pinkerton's academy for young ladies, on
Chiswick Mall, a large family coach, with two fat horses
in blazing harness, driven by a fat coachman in a three-
cornered hat and wig, at the rate of four miles an hour. A
black servant, who reposed on the box beside the fat

coachman, uncurled his bandy legs as soon as the equipage drew up opposite Miss Pinkerton's shining brass plate, and as he pulled the bell, at least a score of young heads were seen peering out of the narrow windows of the stately old brick house.

(Chap. 1)

The definitive first clause, linking the story to the entire era, claims historic sweep and connects the whole century to the teenage girls, Becky Sharp and Amelia Sedley, for whom the coach has come; but it also mocks epic pretentiousness by personifying the century irreverently as a teenager. What then follows previews the qualities that Thackeray would relentlessly satirize as characteristic of his age. We have the heavy stress on material substance ("iron . . . brass . . . brick"), on quantification, on the graceless display of opulence by the socially ambitious, and even on the trappings of imperialism ("black servant"). Implied are the moral flabbiness and ugly physical imbalance that the repeated adjective "fat" connotes. Notice also the almost mechanical behavior of people in this scene. In fact, *"Something mechanical encrusted on the living"* (Bergson's famous definition of the comic, from the end of the century, is a *cri de coeur* of modern life if ever there was one) exactly reflects the feeling of this paragraph and of much of the novel's puppet-like world.

Miss Pinkerton's is really a kind of factory for producing and selling gentility. This refinery has turned out "the Amelia doll," which the Sedley coach comes to collect for that "system of drawing-rooms." Many Victorians believed as an article of faith that upper-class women were meant to preserve and embody civilization. Passive, conventionally good Amelia and scheming, active Becky Sharp, "the Becky puppet" who necessarily "accompanies" her friend, do indeed embody and reflect their civilization, and that is why they matter.

By splitting the protagonist's role into two contrasting female characters, Thackeray made sure that a strong sense of the contradictory nature of life would result. The first chapter ends, "The world is before the two young ladies," and, as chief products of that fallen world, they will mirror it and each other. Becky and Amelia reflect a world of radical incoherence and cultural schism; switching the perspective back and forth between them works metaphorically to give a feeling of life in a society that professes, and makes use of, both a Christian and a "success" ethic but cannot logically reconcile them. These twin nineteenth-century antiheroines project and reflect, of course, deep strains of Thackeray's own personality, particularly the cynicism and sentimentality that he knew existed strongly in himself. But he shrewdly sensed that these figures, coming out of his deepest psychological experience, were types for his whole culture and could thus make clear certain general characteristics of nineteenth-century European society.

They are types, too, of women—or, more precisely, they typify certain influential male conceptions of women as incomplete personalities. Together they synthesize masculine condescension to, and fear of, women. But the joke is that feminine insufficiency and feminine destiny reflect upon men, mimicking their own fates and parodying the stories they tell themselves. To parody is to cast reflections. Amelia is a parody of the myth of goodness, the legend of the patient Griselda, selfless virtue-rewarded-and-rewarding. Becky parodies the myth of advancement and success, the Cinderella-Pamela myth of deserved rise from humble to high station. People actually base their lives on these fictional patterns, but Thackeray finds them sentimental and deceiving. The new Cinderella turns out to be a comic avatar of the wicked stepsister; the new Griselda proves a hapless saint of ignorance and misplaced love. Becky can see reality, but she cannot love. Amelia can love, but cannot see the truth. Together they mime the history and obsessions of that infamous divided self of the nineteenth century.

Amelia is a practicing Christian; Becky is a practicing comedian. Amelia's prayers and simplistic pieties are nearly always shown in a context that points up both their ineffectuality and their intellectual shallowness. Religion does not provide the knowledge and insight of a large and subtle comic vision, but neither does the comic perspective for Thackeray as yet lead to a sustaining faith sufficient to replace Christianity. He reveals, however, in a passage of high significance to my study as well as to *Vanity Fair,* his conviction that the sense of humor has a truly sacred office to perform. After Becky satirizes the Crawley ménage and the hypocrisy of household prayers at old Sir Pitt's, the narrator backs away from her sentiments, but he also names one of her major functions in the comedy:

> You might fancy it was I who was sneering at the practice
> of devotion, which Miss Sharp finds so ridiculous; that it

was I who laughed good-humouredly at the reeling old Silenus of a baronet—whereas the laughter comes from one who has no reverence except for prosperity, and no eye for anything beyond success. Such people there are living and flourishing in the world—Faithless, Hopeless, Charityless: let us have at them, dear friends, with might and main. Some there are, and very successful too, mere quacks and fools: and it was to combat and expose such as those, no doubt, that Laughter was made.

(Chap. 8)

By the end of this paragraph, the purpose of the comic is to establish faith, hope, and charity. Notice the contradictions here: what starts out as a slap at irreverent comedy, a rebuke to Becky, and lip service to established religion concludes by implicitly approving Becky's satire, since it is she who exposes quacks and fools and asserts the moral function of harsh "Laughter." Thackeray, not wanting to appear the foe of organized Christianity, tries to bring comedy under its control, but, through Becky, he cannot help ridiculing it.

III

Becky Sharp is justly one of the most famous characters in fiction. Thackeray made her both the primary agent and object of his comedy and concentrated in her the glamorous vanities of the nineteenth-century Western world. She acts out its restless force, and, miming its magnetic dream of the ambitious self pursuing a career, she performs "all manner of charades," in which we can find reflections of capitalism, Cinderella, Pamela, Napoleon, Thackeray himself, the function of comedy and satire, and much more. "Energy," says Blake, "is eternal delight," and that explains a good deal of Becky's appeal.

She makes the intellectual abstractions of nineteenth-century history live. Take, for instance, this piece by the young Marx, discussing emergent capitalism in the decade of *Vanity Fair's* publication: "Under private property . . . every person speculates on creating a *new* need in another, so as to drive him to a fresh sacrifice, to place him in a new dependence. . . . Each tries to establish over the other an *alien power,* so as thereby to find satisfaction of his own selfish need." Early in *Vanity Fair,* George Osborne is speaking of Dobbin to the ladies in the Sedley house: " 'There's not a finer fellow in the service . . . nor a better officer, though he is not an Adonis, certainly.' And he looked towards the glass himself with much *naïveté,* and in doing so, caught Miss Sharp's eye fixed keenly upon him, at which he blushed a little, and Rebecca thought in her heart, *"Ah, mon beau Monsieur! I think I have your* gage' " (chap. 5). It is a moment of literal reflection, typical of Becky and of the novel. The glass catches a detail that epitomizes and animates a century. Becky exposes the vanity of this world of speculation, but she is the chief speculator. George turns a charitable remark to his own credit, and she decides she can capitalize on his egotism.

She is also Thackeray's reflection upon Napoleon Bonaparte. The main action begins with a comic version of the change from "classic" to "romantic," from *ancien régime* to modern Europe. Becky throws "Johnson's Dixionary," the talismanic gift of the pretentious little Pinkerton hierarchy, right out the window. It is a revolutionary act, desecrating decorum and the authority of the past. Almost immediately she launches a tirade against Miss Pinkerton and shouts to Amelia, *"Vive l'Empereur! Vive Bonaparte!"* (chap. 2). Dr. Johnson is gone; Napoleon rules.

Becky's cry reverberates in the novel and in Thackeray's whole era. In the nineteenth-century imagination Napoleon seemed to personify the apotheosis of individualism, for good or evil. This emperor of personal will fascinated and challenged writers as diverse as Stendhal, Carlyle, Tolstoy, Dostoyevski, and Hardy. His career seemed almost an experiment in modern egoism: how far could the single self go in breaking free of traditional authority, and what did his fate mean? Thackeray continually associates and compares Becky and Napoleon. For example, he refers to Becky as an "upstart" and Bonaparte as the "Corsican upstart" in the same chapter (34). Note, also in chapter 34, "He [Rawdon] believed in his wife as much as the French soldiers in Napoleon." The most striking comparison of all is in Thackeray's drawing of Becky as Napoleon wearing a three-cornered hat and holding her hand under her coat at the opening of chapter 64, "A Vagabond Chapter." If she is a mock Napoleon, he is an overblown Becky Sharp. Her life comments on the hollow vanity of his. Like him, she subverts privilege, exploits the weakness and idiocy of a hereditary aristocracy, manipulates social institutions, and campaigns daringly for victory and success. But, like him, she remains finally a ridiculous prisoner to "this world," a barren St. Helena of self. Thackeray, unlike Stendhal and Dostoyevski, through their respective characters of Julien Sorel and Raskolnikov, makes his meditation on the meaning of Napoleon comic. Becky is a serious judgment on Bonaparte, but she is meant to lampoon all that he stands for. And in Thackeray's comedy we can perhaps see the large implications of comic reflection as a British strategy for dealing with the threatening appeal of amoral personal ambition and worldly power that the French Revolution and Napoleon had symbolized for many.

Becky also acts out the mentality that holds that diamonds are a girl's best friend; however, the person who thinks this way usually becomes like her friends: "Sometimes, when she was away, . . . he [Becky's son, little Rawdon] came into his mother's room. . . . There was the jewel-case, silver-clasped: and the wondrous bronze hand on the dressing table, glistening all over with a hundred rings. . . . O, thou poor lonely little benighted boy! Mother is the name for God in the lips and hearts of little children; and here was one who was worshipping a stone!" (chap. 37). That is not, as it may at first seem, merely sentimental. Thackeray purposely identifies Becky with diamonds and stones, and she mirrors perfectly her society in succumbing to an epidemic of petrifaction.

There is sublime satire in the phrase "a heart of gold," a condition that is often correctly ascribed to whores of all kinds. The Midas touch gilds, then kills. Thackeray mocks himself and his readers in showing how Becky's whorish values permeate our world. She sits in a shambles after Rawdon has cast out Lord Steyne and left her: "The French maid found her. . . . 'Mon Dieu, *Madame,* what has happened?' she asked. What *had* happened? Was she guilty or not? . . . but who could tell what was truth which came from those lips; or if that corrupt heart was in this case pure? All her lies and her schemes, all her selfishness and her wiles, all her wit and genius had come to this bankruptcy" (chap. 53). We are left wondering: Did Steyne get what he paid for? Did he actually have her? Did he possess her?—left wondering, that is, in a manner that makes the sexual act an object for us as well as Becky. This passage has been criticized as equivocal scene-flinching, but it should be read as a subtle and deft satire on what civilization has done to sex. In the history of the world—i.e., Vanity Fair—a woman's sexuality has been transmuted to a possession, a thing on which to capitalize.

IV

Becky defines the way of Thackeray's world. Nearly every passage about her moves explicitly to reduce her life to money or commodity, deadening her vitality. Look carefully at what happens in one of the novel's most famous passages:

> "It isn't difficult to be a country gentleman's wife,"
> Rebecca thought. "I think I could be a good woman if I
> had five thousand a year. I could dawdle about in the
> nursery, and count the apricots on the wall. I could water
> plants in a green-house, and pick off dead leaves from the
> geraniums. I could ask old women about their rheuma-
> tisms, and order half-crown's worth of soup for the
> poor. . . . I could go to church and keep awake in the great
> family pew: or go to sleep behind the curtains, with my
> veil down, if I only had practice. I could pay everybody, if
> I had but the money. . . ." And who knows but Rebecca
> was right in her speculations—and that it was only a ques-
> tion of money and fortune which made the difference be-
> tween her and an honest woman? If you take temptations
> into account, who is to say that he is better than his
> neighbour? A comfortable career of prosperity, if it does
> not make people honest, at least keeps them so. An alder-
> man coming from a turtle feast will not step out of his
> carriage to steal a leg of mutton; but put him to starve, and
> see if he will not purloin a loaf. Becky consoled herself by
> so balancing the chances and equalising the distribution of
> good and evil in the world.
>
> (Chap. 41)

In this first paragraph, the life Becky imagines is not, as Arnold Kettle says, the "worthless" life of Miss Bates; rather, it is the exact life of Emma, and Becky's balanced and witty intelligence here is like Emma's. Only someone who cannot imagine the pleasures of a secure social position or of gardening could find this life simply worthless. Becky, like Emma before her, sees its mixed values—cloying, charming, ridiculous, kindly. She both parodies and expresses her desire for a certain respectable life-style and, in doing so, reveals the tension and ambivalence within a highly intelligent nineteenth-century woman. But as Becky's speculation continues, it takes on a literal and reduced meaning; her knowing irony and sensitivity turn to this: " 'Heigho! I wish I could exchange my position in society, and all my relations for a snug sum in the Three per Cent. Consols'; for so it was that Becky felt the Vanity of human affairs, and it was in those securities that she would have liked to cast anchor" (chap. 42). Notice the play on words: "consoled" becomes "Consols," means become ends, thought and life become ownership, and Becky's mind, unlike Emma's, tends to close out imagination:

> It may perhaps have struck her that to have been honest and humble, to have done her duty, and to have marched straightforward on her way, would have brought her as near happiness as that path by which she was striving to attain it. But,—just as the children at Queen's Crawley went round the room, where the body of their father lay;—if ever Becky had these thoughts, she was accustomed to walk round them, and not look in. She eluded them, and despised them—or at least she was committed to the other path from which retreat was now impossible.
>
> (Chap. 41)

Such virtuous reflections—as that surprising simile proves—are not of "this world," though they occur. They take one out of Vanity Fair, the real reductive world in which Becky must live. The movement of this whole passage is from flexible intelligence to the mechanical operation of the mind. Compare Emma and Becky, those two bold and agile-brained women: one typically moves through the process of reflection and experience to greater knowledge; the other slides into stale, puppet-like speculation. Becky's charming spontaneity habitually metamorphoses into some form of inanimateness or conventional calculation.

What is true of the particular passage is true of the whole book. Becky gets stuck, trapped by the values and life that she herself has exposed as sham. "She has her enemies. Who has not? Her life is her answer to them. She busies herself in works of piety. She goes to church, and never without a footman. Her name is in all the Charity Lists. The Destitute Orange-girl, the Neglected Washerwoman, the Distressed Muffin-man, find in her a fast and generous friend. She is always having stalls at Fancy Fairs for the benefit of these hapless beings" (chap. 67). Becky has been a prime agent in her author's radical criticism of "this world," but she does not wish to change or renounce it. She wants to make the system pay her. Just as Napoleon, despising the crowned heads of Europe and making them wag with fear, nevertheless chose to become one, so Becky, full of spite against the doyennes of propriety, still seeks to assume their roles. Resentment may be the sincerest form of flattery, because it so often leads to imitation.

It is so easy to sentimentalize Becky. (See, for example, Dorothy Van Ghent.) She has—and at special moments even personifies—"good humour," and she carries with her the promise and illusion of freedom. The idea of the career open to talent has fired every liberation movement since the French Revolution, and Becky at times seems to embody that hope. She can prick nerves of feminist sympathy as she rips away stifling conventions. Scorning marriage and motherhood, scheming, gambling, carousing, flaunting sex, joking, meeting setbacks and danger with courage—this behavior can look very much like liberty in a world that smothers or channels the potential of women's lives. But the fact that Becky's career has the scope of a man's makes the failure of her constricting "success" only that much more biting and relevant as satire. Equal opportunity in the age of individualism can lead finally to that gilded cage of hypocrisy, a dull stall in Vanity Fair.

And yet, though she is cast in the role of villainess and mistreats innocent good will, there still *does* seem to be more hope in Becky than in the other characters. Unlike almost all of them, she has the capacity for pleasure, and we see her having the most fun just when she ought to be down and out, disgraced: "Becky had found a little nest;—as dirty a little refuge as ever beauty lay hid in. Becky liked the life. She was at home with everybody in the place, peddlers, punters, tumblers, students and all. She was of a wild, roving nature, inherited from father and mother, who were both Bohemians, by taste and circumstance: if a lord was not by, she would talk to his courier with the greatest pleasure" (chap. 65). This is one of the few times we see somebody happy in *Vanity Fair*. Such a paragraph shows Thackeray groping to imagine a fellowship of outsiders. The feeling and energy here create exactly the same sort of spirit that we find in Robert Burns's *Jolly Beggars* or—sometimes—in twentieth-century countercultures.

One of the fine comic moments in the novel comes when Jos Sedley visits Becky in her disreputable third-rate lodgings. As Jos comes up the stair, "Max" and "Fritz," two students, are trying for an assignation with her:

> "It's you," she said, coming out. "How I have been wait-
> ing for you! Stop! not yet—in one minute you shall come
> in." In that instant she put a rouge-pot, a brandy bottle,
> and a plate of broken meat into the bed, gave one smooth
> to her hair, and finally let in her visitor. . . . And she
> began forthwith to tell her story—a tale so neat, simple,
> and artless, that it was quite evident, from hearing her,
> that if ever there was a white-robed angel escaped from
> heaven to be subject to the infernal machinations and
> villany of fiends here below, that spotless being—that mis-
> erable, unsullied martyr—was present on the bed before
> Jos—on the bed, sitting on the brandy-bottle. . . .
>
> So Becky bowed Jos out of her little garret . . . ; and
> Hans [sic] and Fritz came out of their hole, pipe in mouth,
> and she amused herself by mimicking Jos to them as she
> munched her cold bread and sausage and took draughts of
> her favourite brandy-and-water.
>
> (Chap. 65)

We are beyond good and evil here; for the moment, amoral comic pleasure reigns. Jos somehow deserves what he gets, as Becky puts him on; and her performance for the students sketches both a resentment and a transcendence of circumscribed roles for women. Brains, appetite, frank companionship with men, along with the right and ability to make fun of gross male stupidity, could just possibly be part of a woman's experience.

In chapter 51, Becky, lisping sweet vacuities, sings a song that parodies the sentimentalization of women, "The Rose upon My Balcony":

> The rose upon my balcony the morning air perfuming,
> Was leafless all the winter time and pining for the spring;
> You ask me why her breath is sweet and why her cheek
>   is blooming,
> It is because the sun is out and birds begin to sing.

That song is a takeoff on Amelia and also on woman as a performing object. Becky makes her audience see the *joke* of innocence when it is equated with ignorance and sentimentality. The sticky words of the song explain nothing and communicate nothing true except that such idiocy invites and makes possible a world of exploitation (which is why Thackeray is so ruthlessly satirical toward even well-intentioned dupes and fools). Sentimentality too is a kind of vanity; feeling is showered upon what is hollow, and the one who feels congratulates himself on having fine sentiments and equates good intentions with virtue. Becky's show mimics her society's penchant for self-deception. The sunshine in the song, as it does so often in *Vanity Fair,* reflects the sun that "also rises" in Ecclesiastes on the vain world.

V

Thackeray's habitual parody reflects upon itself and the vanity of human wishes. Amelia shows Dobbin a theme by Georgy, whom she has turned over to old Osborne:

> This great effort of genius, which is still in the possession of George's mother, is as follows:
>
> *On Selfishness.*—Of all the vices which degrade the human character, Selfishness is the most odious and contemptible. An undue love of Self leads to the most monstrous crimes; and occasions the greatest misfortunes both in *States and Families.* As a selfish man will impoverish his family and often bring them to ruin: so a selfish king brings ruin on his people and often plunges them into war.
>
> Example: . . . The selfishness of the late Napoleon Bonaparte occasioned innumerable wars in Europe, and caused him to perish, himself, in a miserable island—that of Saint Helena in the Atlantic Ocean.
>
> We see by these examples that we are not to consult our own interest and ambition, but that we are to consider the interests of others as well as our own.
>
> GEORGE S. OSBORNE
>
> *Athenè House,* 24 *April,* 1827.
>
> "Think of him writing such a hand. . . ," the delighted mother said. "O William," she added, holding out her hand to the Major—"what a treasure Heaven has given me in that boy! . . . he is the image of—of him that's gone!"
>
> (Chap. 58)

I take it that Barbara Hardy had such passages in mind when she wrote that *Vanity Fair* deprives us of "intellectual flattery, moral superiority and emotional indulgence." What starts as a parody of school compositions and youthful naïveté turns out to be a satire on what Joyce would call "the inanity of extolled virtue" and the futility of condemning vice. All literature of valid ethical insight—including *Vanity Fair*—is, from a certain perspective, as absurdly ineffective as Georgy's words in making humanity better: our behavior does not fit our moral knowledge. Saying what is right, we do what is wrong and yet take pride in our beautiful moral sense. The satire mocks the literary imagination, which feeds ethical expectations that mankind can never meet.

The theme and Amelia's response to it both show people uttering truths without knowing what they mean. Georgy's allusion to Napoleon sets off important reverberations, and he concludes with the sum of human wisdom; yet Thackeray has clearly made him a chip off his father's block of selfish vanity. Credulous Amelia becomes crucial. She has no perspective on reality, no way of discriminating between sentiment and fact. When she says that Georgy is the image of George, she has no idea of what she utters. She can only see in the glass of her own defensive idolatry.

Such a moment lets us see why Amelia is such a subtle triumph of characterization and also why she is so unpleasing. Loving, well-meaning, grateful for the sugared lie, gullible and content to be so, she shows us an abiding part of human nature. Historically, most people—certainly most women—for good or ill have resembled Amelia more than Becky and lived lives of visionless quietism. Many more have passively accepted social conventions, have let things happen to them, have moldered in states of intellectual torpor, allowing themselves to be used by the noisy and aggressive, than have tried to shape their lives and put the stamp of their unique being on the world. Amelia naggingly reminds us of that wide sheepish streak in ourselves that asks to be fleeced and that eschews the taxing effort it takes to quit the herd mentality.

Docility has its own forms of vanity. Amelia may not have the magnetism or vitality of Becky, but she has the resonance. Becky's son is merely an object for Becky to use in trying to augment her own worth; she doesn't love him as Amelia loves her boy. And yet, in the proud-mamma passage, look how Amelia, too, turns Georgy into "a treasure" and uses him as a prop to her own vanity. In fact,

Amelia is echoing her own thought, at the time when she agreed to give the boy over to old Osborne, so that he might grow rich: "Her heart and *her treasure*—her joy, hope, love, worship—her God, almost! She must give him up" (chap. 50; italics mine). Thackeray never impugns Amelia's sincerity or the depth of her love, but he shows her worshiping false idols. She makes a commercial bargain that separates her from her son.

What happens to young George of course reflects a pattern in upper-class British life. Boys were separated early from their families. The culture insisted that, if they were to become successful, they must quickly begin to learn the workings of discipline, competition, and power in a masculine environment. Thackeray's closest relationship in life was with his mother, who loved him with Amelia's passion but sent him thousands of miles away from her, back to England from India, when he was six. (That helps account for the idealization of motherhood, the split image between a "good" and "bad" woman, the absence of a mother at crucial times from the lives of Georgy and little Rawdon Crawley, and the pathos the narrator feels for Amelia and for young Rawdon, unloved by his mother.) Becky is a bad mother. She neglects her child, placing ambition and money before maternal love. As an agent of sharp intelligence in the novel, however, she symbolically acts out the Establishment's priority. And we must see that Amelia, though against her will and from purer motives, does exactly the same thing.

Almost against his will, Thackeray distances himself from Amelia and judges her. When Dobbin turns on her and frees himself from his own lifelong obsession, it is climactic:

> "I know what your heart is capable of: it can cling faithfully to a recollection, and cherish a fancy; but it can't feel such an attachment as mine deserves to mate with, and such as I would have won from a woman more generous than you. No, you are not worthy of the love which I have devoted to you. I knew all along that the prize I had set my life on was not worth the winning; that I was a fool, with fond fancies, too, bartering away all of truth and ardour against your little feeble remnant of love. I will bargain no more: I withdraw."
>
> (Chap. 66)

That denunciation is iconoclastic but not antifeminist. Just the opposite: Thackeray shows up as worthless an ideal of womanhood that excludes the full potential of consciousness. He breaks the thrall of the idolatry that equates virtue and ignorance. He criticizes, as Meredith would, what his civilization had done to women and to love.

A few pages later he parodies the happy ending of romantic fiction and the vanities of love in the Western world. Amelia and Dobbin are reunited:

> She was murmuring something about—forgive—dear William—dear, dear, dearest friend—kiss, kiss, kiss, and so forth— . . .
>
> . . . The bird has come in at last. There it is with its head on his shoulder, billing and cooing close up to his heart, with soft outstretched fluttering wings. This is what he has asked for every day and hour for eighteen years. This is what he pined after. Here it is—the summit, the end—the last page of the third volume. Good-bye, Colonel—God bless you, honest William!—Farewell, dear Amelia —Grow green again, tender little parasite, round the rugged old oak to which you cling!
>
> (Chap. 67)

That mocks the idolatrous love dreams of author and audience, especially the powerful illusion that bliss lies in the condition of possessing or being possessed by another. The word "parasite" sets off an explosion of ironical meaning, opening up new perspectives on cultural psychology and history. Amelia is often a painful and ambivalent subject, but, by the end of the novel, Thackeray, letting loose his hostility and satire against her, can fit her into his comic vision.

VI

To recapitulate: Everything in *Vanity Fair* depends on reflecting the great world in the little world of dolls, puppets, artifacts, small histories, and private matters. But this unimposing little world actually radiates with meaning. Superficiality *is* historical reality. Fat Jos Sedley, a fleshbag of conspicuous consumption, mirrors the grotesque side of British imperialism. The mythical minikingdom Pumpernickel, satirized in chapter 64, reflects the farcical history of European nationalism and civilization. Surface is meaning; physical detail reflects the world. The substance, the commodity, the composition of things, characterize life and, by allusion and connotation, also assess it. A high point of Thackeray's mode of reflection comes in the long description in chapter 24—too long to quote in full—of old Osborne's study, its contents, and the relation of the man to his surroundings. The prose makes a whole world come alive:

> Hither Mr. Osborne would retire of a Sunday forenoon when not minded to go to church; and here pass the morning in his crimson leather chair, reading the paper. A couple of glazed book-cases were here, containing standard works in stout gilt bindings. The "Annual Register," the "Gentlemen's Magazine," "Blair's Sermons," and "Hume and Smollett." From year's end to year's end he never took one of these volumes from the shelf; but there was no member of the family that would dare for his life to touch one of the books, except upon those rare Sunday evenings when there was no dinner party, and when the great scarlet Bible and Prayer-book were taken out from the corner where they stood beside his copy of the Peerage, and the servants being rung up to the dining parlour, Osborne read the evening service to his family in a loud grating pompous voice. . . . George as a boy had been horse-whipped in this room many times; his mother sitting sick on the stair listening to the cuts of the whip. The boy was scarcely ever known to cry under his punishment; the poor woman used to fondle and kiss him secretly, and give him money to soothe him when he came out.

Such writing releases huge quantities of meaning from everyday Victorian objects. Here is the crucial passage:

> George's father took the whole of the documents out of the drawer in which he had kept them so long, and locked them into a writing-box, which he tied, and sealed with his seal. Then he opened the book-case, and took down the great red Bible we have spoken of—a pompous book, seldom looked at, and shining all over with gold. There was a frontispiece to the volume, representing Abraham

sacrificing Isaac. Here, according to custom, Osborne had recorded on the fly-leaf, and in his large clerk-like hand, the dates of his marriage and his wife's death, and the births and Christian names of his children. Jane came first, then George Sedley Osborne, then Maria Frances, and the days of the christening of each. Taking a pen, he carefully obliterated George's name from the page; and when the leaf was quite dry, restored the volume to the place from which he had moved it. Then he took a document out of another drawer, where his own private papers were kept; and having read it, crumpled it up and lighted it at one of the candles, and saw it burn entirely away in the grate. It was his will; which being burned, he sat down and wrote off a letter, and rang for his servant, whom he charged to deliver it in the morning. It was morning already: as he went up to bed: the whole house was alight with the sunshine: and the birds were singing among the fresh green leaves in Russell Square.

(Chap. 24)

Old Osborne lives at the center of a system that makes life a ledger; only accounts are real to him. Human will is reified and institutionalized. Religion too is reified and shut up in a book of gold. That frontispiece in the Bible, Osborne's sacrifice of George to Mammon, and George's later death at Waterloo help define a culture by showing that it will trade its children's lives for gold. Casually but firmly, Thackeray alludes to a terrible fact of social life, namely, the existence of human sacrifice, which endures though its forms change. Sensing and expressing links between evangelical religiosity and capitalism, between the heritage of militant British Protestantism and bourgeois righteousness, he condemns, implicitly, stern Jehovah, that capricious, Calvinistic Nobodaddy, on whose terror so much of religion's authority depends. The efficiency, the decorum, the ruthless, quiet power of a mindset on which capitalism and all ideologically triumphant systems have often depended come through in these words. The son has turned into a bad deal that must be liquidated. Thackeray imagines a world—and it is our world—where obliteration may follow on the stroke of a pen.

But the vision and the meaning of the paragraph change radically with the amazing last sentence, which suddenly flashes a comic perspective. There comic faith flourishes. The sunshine plays off the gold, the green leaves mock that pretentious flyleaf, and the tenor of experience is changed. That sunshine, as I said, reflects the sun of Ecclesiastes, and it rises, sets, and shines on an endless flow of being that overwhelms the cruelties and vanities of people or even of civilizations. There is a whole universe of creation that exists beyond the perverse power of men, or even of son-sacrificing, anthropomorphic gods, to control or ruin it. Inner and outer life seem totally alienated, and that may be lucky, since Osborne's murderous wrath cannot stop the rising sun, the coming of spring, or the instinctive gaiety of being. The writing shows that a human mind can imagine the meaning of the sunshine and project a god's-eye vision—or, more accurately, a perspective from the revolving sun—which comprehends the alienation of Osborne, the follies of society, and the vanity of human wishes. That final sentence mocks solipsism and even cultural chauvinism: the mood of the individual and the values of a ruling class are not universal. The religion of gold pales in the sunshine, and vitality returns. "Moralise as we will, the world goes on." The switch in perspective reflects a comic vision and gives intimations of a kind of immortality: suddenly I see the sun and its spawn of natural existence, and I sense a fertile resource of mind that can perceive the almost infinite variety and wonder of ontology, even at a moment of spiritual death.

Strategies in *Vanity Fair*

H. M. Daleski

The opening sentence of *Vanity Fair* scarcely prepares us for the astonishing handling of point of view which characterizes the novel as a whole. It is not only "the famous little Becky Puppet" that may be said to be "uncommonly flexible in the joints" but the narrative method, and this results in the kind of virtuoso display that the "Manager of the Performance" could equally have taken pride in. The opening sentence, however, accords comfortably enough with our sense of how stories are conventionally told in Victorian fiction: "While the present century was in its teens, and on one sunshiny morning in June, there drove up to the great iron gate of Miss Pinkerton's academy for young ladies, on Chiswick Mall, a large family coach, with two fat horses in blazing harness, driven by a fat coachman in a three-cornered hat and wig, at the rate of four miles an hour." That the narrator is omniscient is at once communicated by that precise "four miles an hour," and the rich particularity of time and place and circumstance seems designed to evoke a factual, "objective" view of the setting. The objectivity, a concomitant of this type of omniscience, seems also to be a function of the narrator's taking a god's-eye view of the scene, and thus of his having assumed a position outside the fictional world. He distances himself still further by locating his story at a point in time remote from that in which he is living. The narrative mode, therefore, appears to be that

From *Unities: Studies in the English Novel.* © 1985 by the University of Georgia Press.

of a detached, impersonal omniscience; but before the end of the first short chapter there is a decided change of method.

Far from maintaining a posture of impersonality, the narrator speedily begins to refer to himself in the first person; and though, to judge by the opening sentence, he has been at pains to establish the existential solidity of what he is depicting, he is soon insisting on its fictionality and on his own status as novelist:

> But as we are to see a great deal of Amelia, there is no harm in saying, at the outset of our acquaintance, that she was a dear little creature; and a great mercy it is, both in life and in novels, which (and the latter especially) abound in villains of the most sombre sort, that we are to have for a constant companion so guileless and good-natured a person. As she is not a heroine, there is no need to describe her person; indeed I am afraid that her nose was rather short than otherwise.

The posture of omniscience that the narrator adopts here may be described—in contradistinction to that referred to above—as both personal and self-conscious. Instances of such self-consciousness abound in the novel, but I shall quote only two further representative examples:

> If, a few pages back, the present writer claimed the privilege of peeping into Miss Amelia Sedley's bedroom, and understanding with the omniscience of the novelist all the gentle pains and passions which were tossing upon that innocent pillow, why should he not declare himself to be Rebecca's confidante too, master of her secrets, and sealkeeper of that young woman's conscience?

> As his hero and heroine pass the matrimonial barrier, the novelist generally drops the curtain, as if the drama were over then: the doubts and struggles of life ended: as if, once landed in the marriage country, all were green and pleasant there: and wife and husband had nothing to do but to link each other's arms together, and wander gently downwards towards old age in happy and perfect fruition. But our little Amelia was just on the bank of her new country, and was already looking anxiously back towards the sad

friendly figures waving farewell to her across the stream, from the other distant shore.

It is not the practice of "the novelist" that we are enjoined to consider but that of other novelists; and it is not "our little Amelia" whom we are urged to identify as different but our novelist, as he pursues a new realism in the presentation of marriage.

The narrator, however, slides back as easily into a posture of impersonal objectivity; and so in the first chapter, for instance, his reflections about "life and . . . novels" and the sort of description that is appropriate to a nonheroine coexist happily with his vivid, scenic rendering of the confrontation between Miss Pinkerton and her sister over the question of a present for Becky Sharp or of the way the latter flings the dictionary back at the startled feet of Miss Jemima. As early as chapter 1, therefore, it seems that, if omniscience is the chosen narrative method, it is a particularly flexible kind of omniscience, modulating freely from the impersonal to the personal, from the dramatic to the confidential, and from the detached to the self-conscious. But in fact (as we shall see) omniscience turns out to be only one of the major narrative stances that the novelist adopts.

The narrator's omniscience, moreover, is itself put in question, though he is given to drawing attention to it. He declares his omniscience, for instance, in the passage already quoted in which he refers to the passions and secrets of the two young ladies whose story he is telling. And periodically he reminds us of the fact: apropos of his telling us that Joseph Sedley thinks "a great deal" about Becky, he remarks parenthetically that "novelists have the privilege of knowing everything"; and he explains his being "in a situation to be able to tell the public how Crawley and his wife lived without any income," by remarking that "the novelist, it has been said before, knows everything." In fact, however, the narrator does not appear to know everything: "I wonder," he says, "whether [Miss Crawley] knew it was not only Becky who wrote the letters, but that Mrs. Rawdon actually took and sent home the trophies—which she bought for a few francs. . . . The novelist, who knows everything, knows this also. Be this, however, as it may." He may know that it is Becky who procures and sends the trophies, but he does not seem to know whether Miss Crawley knows this or not. Miss Crawley, indeed, seems to be altogether beyond him, for when she meets Rawdon at Brighton, the narrator says, "I don't know whether Miss Crawley had any private feelings of regard or emotion upon seeing her old favourite; but she held out a couple of fingers to him." On other occasions it is Amelia who seems to be beyond his ken, for he admits that he does not know what her thoughts are, and that he "cannot explain the meaning" of a particularly striking act of hers. The narrator's admission, in certain situations, of his own limited knowledge is thus also a recurrent feature of the narrative. Accordingly, the most famous (or infamous) example of such an admission—the narrator's uncertainty about Becky's guilt when her husband finds her in compromising circumstances with Lord Steyne: "What *had* happened? Was she guilty or not? She said not; but who could tell what was truth which came from those lips; or if that corrupt heart was in this case pure?"—should not be viewed in isolation as an epitome of the novelist's cowardly evasiveness but seen as an integral part of a calculated narrative strategy, a consistent inconsistency.

Unlike the changes of role that the narrator adopts within the overall play of omniscience, a regular shift of focus (in Gérard Genette's sense) within the fictional world may be regarded as a conventional feature of most omniscient narrative, especially the massive Victorian variety such as *Vanity Fair* or *Our Mutual Friend* or *Middlemarch,* in which there are a large number of focal characters. This kind of shift, however, has by itself been found to be dizzy-making in *Vanity Fair:* "Thackeray," say Geoffrey and Kathleen Tillotson, "turns from one personage to another and sometimes so quickly that we grow giddy unless we keep pace by reading slowly." It seems to me that we easily accept such shifts of focus because we are used to encountering them in other novels too, and in this novel we are anyway preoccupied with the narrator's own transformations. The combined effect of these variations of narrative mode and focus, however, is to establish a general fluidity that facilitates radical movements away from the fictional world itself. For in *Vanity Fair* there are, in addition, repeated shifts of dimension, shifts from the fictional to the real world.

We may distinguish, in this regard, five kinds of shift. First, there is the shift from the fictional world to the putative real world of the reader—and to his imagined response to fictional events. Sometimes the shift of dimension that is forced on us in such cases is so sharp that it is subversive of the dramatic action that is in progress, suddenly cutting it short, as in the following account of the events that lead to Dobbin's famous fight with Cuff: " 'Take that, you little devil!' cried Mr. Cuff, and down came the wicket again on the child's hand—Don't be horrified, ladies, every boy at a public school has done it. Your children will so do and be done by, in all probability—Down came the wicket again; and Dobbin started up." The narrator seems here to be at least as much concerned with his readers as his characters, and makes us shift our attention accordingly. Sometimes the shift is occasioned by the narrator's apparent wish to justify his fiction to an imagined critical reader, as when he tells us of the response Amelia evokes in those close to George Osborne:

> After every one of her visits (and oh how glad she was when they were over!) Miss Osborne and Miss Maria Osborne, and Miss Wirt, the vestal governess, asked each other with increased wonder, "What *could* George find in that creature?"
>
> How is this? some carping reader exclaims. How is it that Amelia, who had such a number of friends at school, and was so beloved there, comes out into the world and is spurned by her discriminating sex! My dear sir, there were no men at Miss Pinkerton's establishment except the old dancing-master; and you would not have had the girls fall out about *him?*

And sometimes the narrator turns from the fiction to the reader in order (ironically) to defend something he has *not* done in the narrative:

> A polite public will no more bear to read an authentic description of vice than a truly refined English or American female will permit the word breeches to be pronounced in her chaste hearing. And yet, Madam, both are walking the world before our faces every day, without much shocking us. If you were to blush every time they went by, what complexions you would have! It is only when their naughty names are called out that your modesty has any occasion to show alarm or sense of outrage, and it has been the wish of the present writer, all through this story, deferentially to submit to the fashion at present prevailing, and only to hint at the existence of wickedness in a light,

easy, and agreeable manner, so that nobody's fine feelings may be offended.

Second, there are shifts from the fictional world to the putative real world of the reader in which attention is directed not to his response to the fiction but to his own imagined conduct in the real world. Describing how the rich Miss Crawley exploits the people round her, the narrator first generalizes from her behavior, and then, in a sudden shift, turns the generalization on the reader:

> Gratitude among certain rich folks is scarcely natural or to be thought of. They take needy people's services as their due. Nor have you, O poor parasite and humble hanger-on, much reason to complain! Your friendship for Dives is about as sincere as the return which it usually gets. It is money you love, and not the man; and were Croesus and his footman to change places, you know, you poor rogue, who would have the benefit of your allegiance.

Sometimes the narrator changes focus as well as dimension, includes himself as well as the reader in the criticism that is voiced, and (confounding confusion) details an imagined response in the supposed real world to an event that is actually taking place in the fictional world—as when he remarks how everyone attends Lord Steyne's parties: "In a word, everybody went to wait upon this great man—everybody who was asked: as you the reader (do not say nay) or I the writer hereof would go if we had an invitation." The moralizing note in a number of these exhortations to the reader becomes frankly hortatory on occasion, as when Miss Crawley's illness is depicted: "Picture to yourself, O fair young reader, a worldly, selfish, graceless, thankless, religionless old woman, writhing in pain and fear, and without her wig. Picture her to yourself, and ere you be old, learn to love and pray."

Third, the narrator also generalizes from specific fictional incidents not in order to turn his satire on the reader but to establish universal principles of being, drawing us once again, however, from the fiction to life in the supposed real world. This, for instance, is how he moves from Becky to "the world" in which she figures in the fiction, and then to "the world" in which he and his readers live: "Miss Rebecca was not, then, in the least kind or placable. All the world used her ill, said this young misanthropist, and we may be pretty certain that persons whom all the world treats ill deserve entirely the treatment they get. The world is a looking-glass, and gives back to every man the reflection of his own face." The shifts in dimension become more complex when the general truth that is elicited from the fiction and applied to the real world is then subsequently disproved in the fiction. The narrator makes this comment, for instance, after he has described how Becky seeks to inveigle Jos Sedley into marriage when she first meets him: "And this I set down as a positive truth. A woman with fair opportunities, and without an absolute hump, may marry WHOM SHE LIKES"—but he thereafter proceeds to show how the attractive Becky loses her opportunity. Sometimes the narrator, moving from his specific fictional world to the world at large by means of a generalizing comment, contrives at the same time (through a deft use of parenthesis, which—as we shall see—is one of his most effective narrative weapons) to narrow the focus to the more restricted domain of the British reader and his foibles:

> There is little doubt that old Osborne believed all he said, and that the girls were quite earnest in their protestations of affection for Miss Swartz. People in Vanity Fair fasten on to rich folks quite naturally. If the simplest people are disposed to look not a little kindly on great Prosperity (for I defy any member of the British public to say that the notion of Wealth has not something awful and pleasing to him; and you, if you are told that the man next to you at dinner has got a half a million, not to look at him with a certain interest); if the simple look benevolently on money, how much more do your old worldlings regard it! Their affections rush out to meet and welcome money.

Fourth, there are a number of shifts from the fictional world to the real, real world—that is to say, not to a real world of imagined readers but of historic personages. Such a shift is made as early as chapter 2, following Becky's defiant rejection of the dictionary at the end of the previous chapter:

> Miss Sedley was almost as flurried at the act of defiance as Miss Jemima had been; for, consider, it was but one minute that she had left school, and the impressions of six years are not got over in that space of time. Nay, with some

persons those awes and terrors of youth last for ever and
ever. I know, for instance, an old gentleman of sixty-
eight, who said to me one morning at breakfast, with a
very agitated countenance, "I dreamed last night that I was
flogged by Dr. Raine." Fancy had carried him back five-
and-fifty years in the course of that evening. Dr. Raine and
his rod were just as awful to him in his heart, then, at
sixty-eight, as they had been at thirteen.

With regard to the reference to Dr. Raine, J. I. M. Stewart tells us
that Matthew Raine served as headmaster of Charterhouse from 1791
until 1811. Though Thackeray himself did not go to this school until
1822, the anecdote in the novel is based on a real-life experience, as
an 1841 letter to Edward FitzGerald, which describes the dream of
the "old gentleman," indicates: "The old fellow is 65 years old, and
told me that only that night he had a dream about being flogged at
Charter-House — There is something touching in this I think about
which Mr. William Wordsworth might make a poem if he chose."
Was it forgetfulness, we wonder, that made Thackeray some six
years after the letter (when he wrote the first monthly number of the
novel) change the old fellow's age from 65 to 68—or a wish, for all
his deliberate shifts of dimension, to assert the autonomy of his
fiction? Certainly, in other instances the fiction absorbs the real world,
as it were, when the shift is made in the course of a single sentence,
and the back-and-forth movement between worlds is so quick it
almost escapes the eye: "The curses to which the General gave a low
utterance, as soon as Rebecca and her conqueror had quitted him,
were so deep, that I am sure no compositor in Messrs. Bradbury and
Evans's establishment would venture to print them were they written down. They came from the General's heart." Bradbury and
Evans, of course, were Thackeray's publishers.

Fifth, some shifts to the real world are made by way of reference
not to historic personages but to the narrator's projecting himself as
the historic novelist, engaging, under the pressure of the fiction, in
something very like personal reminiscence. When Dobbin is left
alone at Vauxhall, for instance, we are told: "It wasn't very good fun
for Dobbin—and, indeed, to be alone at Vauxhall, I have found,
from my own experience, to be one of the most dismal sports ever
entered into by a bachelor." Similarly, in deliberating on the effect of
rack punch on the destinies of his characters, the narrator says: "To

this truth I can vouch as a man; there is no headache in the world like that caused by Vauxhall punch. Through the lapse of twenty years, I can remember the consequence of two glasses!—two wine glasses!—but two, upon the honour of a gentleman; and Joseph Sedley, who had a liver complaint, had swallowed at least a quart of the abominable mixture." But the narrator's most audacious sleight of hand in this regard is a shift (signaled by a parenthesis) to the world of the historic novelist which draws with it the transformation of a character into something like a real-life personage, though this sudden life is speedily collapsed into the fiction. The narrator recounts how Jos Sedley presents "two handsome nosegays of flowers" to Amelia and Becky:

> "Thank you, dear Joseph," said Amelia, quite ready to kiss her brother, if he were so minded. (And I think for a kiss from such a dear creature as Amelia, I would purchase all Mr. Lee's conservatories out of hand.)
> "Oh heavenly, heavenly flowers!" exclaimed Miss Sharp.

No editor that I am aware of has established the identity of Mr. Lee, but it would seem to me not unreasonable to assume that his conservatories were well known in Thackeray's day—the more especially since we are almost at once informed by Jos that he has bought his flowers "at Nathan's."

What the narrative steadily encompasses, therefore, are changes of focus, as it moves from one focal character to another (as the Tillotsons remarked); transformations of the narrator, as he moves from one role to another; and shifts of dimension, as we are made to move from one world to another. But the novelist's most striking innovation is his threefold changing of the position from which the narrator views the fictional world. The method, in this respect, is far more revolutionary than that employed in Dickens's *Bleak House* (published a few years after *Vanity Fair*), in which there are two alternating narratives, for they are separate narratives (even though they overlap) and there are two separate narrators, the omniscient narrator and Esther Summerson, the first-person protagonist-narrator. In *Vanity Fair* there is only one narrative and only one narrator (for all his transformations), but the fictional world is viewed from three distinct and separate positions, not two, as in *Bleak House*. The first position that the narrator takes up is outside the fictional world;

and all the examples of his procedures that I have referred to so far are variants of the flexible omniscience that characterizes this major stance. But he also takes up a position inside the fictional world.

The first instance of the narrator's change of position comes in chapter 22 after some two hundred pages of omniscient narrative, and it is signaled by a quietly deceptive parenthesis. The narrator is describing Amelia's marriage to George in a manner that we are by now thoroughly accustomed to:

> In a word, George had thrown the great cast. He was going to be married. Hence his pallor and nervousness— his sleepless night and agitation in the morning. I have heard people who have gone through the same thing own to the same emotion. After three or four ceremonies, you get accustomed to it, no doubt; but the first dip, everybody allows, is awful.
>
> The bride was dressed in a brown silk pelisse (as Captain Dobbin has since informed me), and wore a straw bonnet with a pink ribbon.

The shift here is outrageous. If previously the validity of the narrative has been based on the narrator's privileged omniscience (though this, as we have seen, is on occasion unaccountably limited), it is now made a matter of information which the narrator directly amasses within the fictional world itself. No longer taking a god's-eye view, which enables him to penetrate into the thoughts of a Becky or Amelia, he is lending an all too human ear to what Dobbin tells him. And yet, though he is now a distinct presence in the fictional world, a man whom Dobbin can talk to, he is quite without substance, remaining the same unnamed, unparticularized figure whom we have encountered in the omniscient narrative. Though he is clearly not a Marlow recounting the story of Lord Jim and himself playing a part in it, technically he is here transformed into an observer-narrator. This transformation might be expected to split the novel in two; but since it does not, we are forced to conclude that all that has happened is that the narrator we have known to this point has merely changed his position, stealthily slipping (in that parenthesis) into the fictional world from outside it.

Nor is this a random occurrence. From here on the novel is steadily punctuated by illicit border crossings. The narrator is "told by Dr. Pestler (now a most flourishing lady's physician . . .), that

[Amelia's] grief at weaning the child was a sight that would have unmanned a Herod"; he declares Dobbin was mistaken in seeing a resemblance to Amelia in "a figure in a book of fashions": "I have seen it, and can vouch that it is but the picture of a high-waisted gown with an impossible doll's face simpering over it"; he has a special "informant," who "knows everything" and is appropriately named Tom Eaves, and it is Tom who shows him Gaunt House: " 'The Prince and Perdita have been in and out of that door, sir,' he has often told me"; and he relates that "the before-mentioned Tom Eaves (who has no part in this history, except that he knew all the great folks in London, and the stories and mysteries of each family) had further information regarding my Lady Steyne, which may or may not be true," but he proceeds to provide it (in Tom Eaves's name, of course). It is, however, at the very end of the novel, in the section which is set at Pumpernickel, that the narrator begins positively to obtrude his observer status on us: "Georgy was always present at the play, but it was the Major who put Emmy's shawl on after the entertainment. . . . It was on this very tour that I, the present writer of a history of which every word is true, had the pleasure to see them first, and to make their acquaintance." This statement now challenges some major suppositions in the omniscient narrative. Though we, in keeping with the convention, have been ready to take the omniscient narrator's word for the truth of his narrative, he (as we have seen) has been at pains to insist over and over on its fictionality; now, though we may be inclined to believe that an observer-narrator may possibly be unreliable, and though he indeed on occasion purveys information which "may or may not be true," he here categorically asserts the absolute truth of his narrative. Further contradictions speedily materialize. It appears that, at Pumpernickel, it is the observer-narrator who will conduct the narrative, for he takes over at the point at which he first sees Dobbin and his party, and the rest of this chapter is full of references to his direct observation of them at the opera, especially Amelia ("I suppose it was because it was predestined that I was to write this particular lady's memoirs that I remarked her"). The omniscient narrator, however, returns in the next chapter and maintains his presence to the end, though the observer-narrator intrudes into his narrative on a number of occasions. Furthermore, though the observer-narrator does a lot of watching at the opera, he seems in general to be more of a listener than an observer, and it becomes evident that his narrative ("of which every word is true")—*the* whole narrative of *Vanity Fair* if we accept his claims—is certainly second-hand and possibly unreliable. One half of it, that relating to Amelia and her circle, is based, we must assume, on what he is told by an interested party; for it is Dobbin (who, we remember, informed him what Amelia wore at her wedding) who presumably gives him that piece of information, together with other details of her history, at Pumpernickel, where they first make acquaintance. And the other half, that relating to Becky and her circle, is based on mere gossip:

> William, in a state of great indignation, though still un-aware of all the treason that was in store for him, walked about the town wildly until he fell upon the Secretary of Legation, Tapeworm, who invited him to dinner. As they were discussing that meal, he took occasion to ask the Secretary whether he knew anything about a certain Mrs. Rawdon Crawley, who had, he believed, made some noise in London; and then Tapeworm, who of course knew all the London gossip, and was besides a relative of Lady Gaunt, poured out into the astonished Major's ears such a history about Becky and her husband as astonished the querist, and supplied all the points of this narrative, for it was at that very table years ago that the present writer had the pleasure of hearing the tale. Tufto, Steyne, the Crawleys, and their history—everything connected with Becky and her previous life, passed under the record of the bitter diplomatist.

Nor is the novelist content with these maneuvers. A narrator, ordinarily speaking, may occupy one or other of two major positions in relation to his narrative: he may be inside or outside the fictional world. Thackeray not only shows how this choice may not necessarily be exclusive but invents a third possibility:

> Sir Pitt had an unmarried half-sister who inherited her mother's large fortune. . . . She had signified . . . her intention of leaving her inheritance between Sir Pitt's second son and the family at the Rectory. . . . Miss Crawley was, in consequence, an object of great respect when she came to Queen's Crawley, for she had a balance at her banker's which would have made her beloved anywhere.

What a dignity it gives an old lady, that balance at the banker's! How tenderly we look at her faults if she is a relative (and may every reader have a score of such), what a kind good-natured old creature we find her! How the junior partner of Hobbs and Dobbs leads her smiling to the carriage with the lozenge upon it. . . . How, when she comes to pay us a visit, we generally find an opportunity to let our friends know her station in the world! We say (and with perfect truth) I wish I had Miss MacWhirter's signature to a cheque for five thousand pounds. She wouldn't miss it, says your wife. She is my aunt, say you, in an easy careless way, when your friend asks if Miss MacWhirter is any relative. Your wife is perpetually sending her little testimonies of affection, your little girls work endless worsted baskets, cushions, and footstools for her. . . . Ah, gracious powers! I wish you would send me an old aunt—a maiden aunt—an aunt with a lozenge on her carriage, and a front of light coffee-coloured hair—how my children should work workbags for her, and my Julia and I would make her comfortable! Sweet—sweet vision! Foolish—foolish dream!

The first paragraph of this passage is clearly part of the omniscient narrative, and its satirical point is simple and concisely expressed in its last sentence. What is puzzling is why the novelist elaborates the same (simple) satirical point in the second paragraph, and at much greater length (thirty-three lines as opposed to the first eleven lines in the full printed text) in relation to characters we have not yet met; and we therefore wonder too what sort of narrative this is. At first, when the narrator turns to the reader and directly addresses him, it seems that we have here yet another instance, familiar enough by this point in the narrative, of a shift of dimension (from the fictional to the real world) which is designed to force the reader to contemplate his own conduct. It is the junior partner of Hobbs and Dobbs and Miss MacWhirter who give us pause. Who exactly are they? If they make their appearance in the same fictional dimension as the reader, namely, the putative real world, are they then historic personages like Dr. Raine? Clearly not. Are they then fictional characters, like Sir Pitt and Miss Crawley and the family at the Rectory? Equally clearly not, for they make no further appearance in *Vanity Fair*, and even here have little existence apart from their names. And where is it, then—in what realm, as it were—that they do make their appearance? If it is neither the real world, for they are not real like Dr. Raine, nor the fictional world, for they have no part whatsoever in the story of Amelia and Becky (and Miss Crawley), we can only conclude that they have their being (such as it is) in an amorphous area that is insinuated in between the fictional and real worlds. They are not so much fictional characters (whom the omniscient narrator sometimes refers to as puppets) as dummies, who are no more than their names, and whom the novelist places in a shadow (fictional) world that he creates to mediate between the real world and the (real) fictional world. It is as if the fictional world casts long shadows out to this world and so gains in solidity, for the way in which Miss Crawley is treated at Queen's Crawley is validated, so to speak, by the analogous treatment of Miss MacWhirter. At the same time the reader is satirized for being as ready to fawn on his rich aunt as Miss Crawley's relatives are on her. But if that is the case, then the reader, in this instance, is also not situated in the real world but coexists with Miss MacWhirter. And who, then, is the "I" who makes his appearance (with his Julia and his children) at the end of the passage? He is not the historic Thackeray, whose wife was not named Julia; he is not the omniscient narrator, who has so often addressed the reader, for he has here taken up a position in the shadow world of Miss MacWhirter; for the same reason, he is not the observer-narrator who exists in the world of Amelia and Dobbin and Becky; he is not even an incarnation of the implied author, whom we may take to abhor the "I's" sycophantic values. This "I" is a dummy-narrator, a nominal fictional projection of the novelist, whom he places in the shadow fictional world for satirical purposes: the satirical attack is pressed home (in a manner that recalls "A Modest Proposal") by having a dummy-narrator take the obnoxious values for granted. The novelist, we see, has contrived to invent a third narratorial position: neither inside the fictional world nor outside it in the ordinary omniscient sense, it is somewhere in between.

The novelist makes extensive use of the shadow world, but one further example of this should suffice. I quote the following passage both because it is also charmingly exemplary of the humor with which Thackeray often camouflages his tactical narrative moves, and because it indicates in addition another dimension of the Vanity Fair image: Vanity Fair is the world in which Becky and Amelia live; it is also the world in which the novelist and his readers live; and it is amenable too, as here, to projection in the shadow world. This is how the novelist satirically emphasizes the extent of Becky's chagrin at being unable to marry Sir Pitt because she is already married to his son:

> I remember one night being in the Fair myself, at an evening party. I observed Old Miss Toady . . . single out for her special attentions and flattery little Mrs. Briefless, the barrister's wife, who . . . is as poor as poor can be.
>
> What, I asked in my own mind, can cause this obsequiousness on the part of Miss Toady . . . ? Miss Toady explained presently . . . "You know," she said, "Mrs. Briefless is granddaughter of Sir John Redhand, who is so ill . . . that he can't last six months. Mrs. Briefless's papa succeeds; so you see she *will* be a baronet's daughter." And Toady asked Briefless and his wife to dinner the very next week.
>
> If the mere chance of becoming a baronet's daughter can procure a lady such homage in the world, surely, surely we may respect the agonies of a young woman who has lost the opportunity of becoming a baronet's wife.

The foregoing account should give some idea of the richness of the narrative method in *Vanity Fair,* but the mixture of effects (insofar as these have been noted at all) is not to everyone's taste, and has in fact been the object of strong criticism by two well-known critics. Dorothy Van Ghent, for instance, refers first to the comment, "If Miss Rebecca can get the better of *him* [that is, Jos], and at her first entrance into life, she is a young person of no ordinary cleverness," and then to the passage (which I have previously quoted) in which the narrator, in what she calls an "unforgivable parenthesis," expresses a desire to kiss Amelia:

> What we feel is that two orders of reality are clumsily getting in each other's way: the order of imaginative reality, where Becky lives, and the order of historical reality, where William Makepeace Thackeray lives. The fault becomes more striking in the . . . unforgivable parenthesis. . . . The picture of Thackeray himself kissing Amelia pulls Amelia quite out of the created world of *Vanity Fair*

and drops her into some shapeless limbo of Thackerayan sentiment where she loses all aesthetic orientation.

It seems to me, however, that the shifts from one order of reality to the other are so pervasive that we become quite habituated to them; and, moreover, as I have tried to show, that they are smoothly supportive of the imaginative reality by repeatedly offering a validation of it in other terms. As for that wished-for kiss, I have also argued that "the created world of *Vanity Fair*" consists steadily of three worlds, what I have called the real fictional world, the shadow fictional world, and the fictional real world; and consequently it seems to me more accurate to say that Amelia (in that offensive parenthesis), far from being left in some limbo, is pulled out of the fictional world into the real world for a moment—and then returned to her natural habitat with no apparent ill effects. Magicians, if they are skillful enough, get away with such things.

Another influential critic, Wolfgang Iser, objects to further aspects of the method:

> [The narrator's] reliability is . . . reduced by the fact that he is continually donning new masks: at one moment he is an observer of the Fair, like the reader; then he is suddenly blessed with extraordinary knowledge, . . . "knowing everything"; and then, toward the end, he announces that . . . he overheard [the whole story] in a conversation.

> The "Manager of the Performance" opens up a whole panorama of views on the reality described, which can be seen from practically every social and human standpoint. The reader is offered a host of different perspectives, and so is almost continually confronted with the problem of how to make them consistent.

It seems to me, however, that what is at issue is not the narrator's change of masks (if he may indeed be thought of as "continually donning" new ones) but position, and that his changes of position do not affect the reliability of what he reports. The observer-narrator's presentation of Amelia and her party in Pumpernickel, for instance, is no less (and no more) reliable than the omniscient narrator's account of their journey to Pumpernickel. Furthermore, I think that Iser creates an unnecessary problem for the reader when he implies that his only recourse, in face of the "host of different perspectives" that confront him, is to try "to make them consistent." I trust it has become evident in the previous discussion that it is quite impossible to reconcile the contradictions thrown up by the narrative, to account satisfactorily, for example, for the narrator's being both omniscient and limited in his knowledge, or for his being able—quite against nature and the laws of fiction—to be both inside and outside the fictional world and in a third position as well. All we can do is accept the blatant inconsistencies. But we might do well to ask why it is that a novelist, who in this very work proves himself to be a master of his craft, should go out of his way to force inconsistencies on us.

I believe this question should be related to another aspect of the narrative. *Vanity Fair* is a revolutionary novel—for its times—in a further respect: it is a novel without a plot. In abandoning plot (in the sense of a single, encompassing, causally connected action), Thackeray gave up the traditional (and conventional Victorian) mechanism for unifying his material; and he compounded his difficulty by deciding to have two major protagonists, Becky and Amelia, for this deprived him as well of a single, steady center. It is true that through a skillful use of a principle of contrast in his handling of Becky and Amelia (and of the characters who surround them), Thackeray manages to balance one part of the novel against the other and so achieve a modicum of unity; but, as J. Y. T. Greig has pointed out, the principle (which he describes earlier) is not maintained throughout: "*Vanity Fair* is unified and shapely up to . . . the Battle of Waterloo . . . It becomes unified and shapely again after chapter 43 (Pumpernickel) . . . But in between—roughly 300 pages—the plot of the first and last sections of the book is suspended, and the unity of the novel disappears. Two stories now occupy the author's attention alternately." The unity of the novel, as this is established through the working of contrast, no doubt disappears in the way Greig claims it does; but this is not to say it lacks all unity. For, paradoxically enough, the narrative method ensures that it should be apprehended as a whole. We might expect that the various inconsistencies of the method would fragment the novel in chaotic disruptions of effect; but in fact they help to bind it together. In theory the observer-narrator should, as it were, cancel out the omniscient narrator, who anyway repeatedly undermines his own status both by denying his omniscience and by leading a surreptitious dummy existence. In practice, however, each merges into the other, for throughout we have only one speaker: we hear only one (immediately recognizable) voice; and we never doubt that all along we have only one narrator, whose solidity is increased, not diminished, by the successfully encompassed contradictions—and whose pervasive and dominating presence is a cohesive force. Similarly, we know that what at times seems like three narratives is actually and throughout only one, and our awareness of its oneness, of a wholeness which successfully holds together and subsumes its three constituent parts, is productive of a greater sense of its unity than that lent it by even an effective use of contrast. Furthermore, the constant shifts from the fictional world to the real world and also to the shadow fictional world ensure that we perceive the fictional world as a separate entity, one that—for all its multifariousness—is apprehended as a unified whole when it is compared, in its own distinctness, with another order of existence. There is method, we come to see, in the narrative madness.

II

It is the novelist's imaginative sense of his subject, however, more even than his technical intuition, that produces the imagery which unifies *Vanity Fair* at a more profound level. It might be thought that it is the image of Vanity Fair—which Thackeray, nicely exemplifying an awareness of the phenomenon of intertextuality that so enthralls us today, lifts straight out of Bunyan—that effectively binds the novel together. This, to a degree, is the case since the society that is depicted in the novel *is* the Fair, is located in it; and in all its varied manifestations it gives repeated embodiment to the values of the Fair, to the materialism and sensuality which are its most marked features in Bunyan, and to the "humbugs and falsenesses and pretensions" which Thackeray adds to Bunyan. The novel consequently has great thematic concentration, asserting over and over that, in a society whose only values are the world and the flesh, "all is vanity." But the Fair, even in Bunyan and more so in the novel, is an intellectual construct rather than an image; and its lack of concrete particularity reduces its force. As an image it was probably of more significance to the novelist than it is now to the reader. To the novelist, we may be inclined to believe, it may have served—during the process of composition—as a species of scaffolding, encompassing the structure that was slowly taking shape, and enabling it to be built. But, like scaffolding, it remains external, and once the structure exists may be dispensed with. As an image in the finished work it certainly is secondary, and a different image animates the whole from within and binds it together. Whereas the idea of Vanity Fair may be regarded as having shaped the novelist's sense of his subject, it is his imaginative conception of the subject which generates the binding image.

The image arises naturally out of the setting of the novel, though this has been taken to be merely incidental to its main concerns: *"Vanity Fair,"* say Geoffrey and Kathleen Tillotson, "is not primarily a 'historical' novel . . . because, unlike a truly historical novel, it owes nothing essential to the time of its action . . . *Vanity Fair* deals first and foremost in human nature, and without essential loss, could be set in any time, past, present, or future." We have only to compare *Vanity Fair* with *The History of Henry Esmond* to agree that it is not a historical novel; and it seems reasonable to believe that the society portrayed in it is, in essentials, that of Thackeray's own day. But that is not to say that it "owes nothing essential" to its setting. The fact that Thackeray chose to set his novel at the time of the Battle of Waterloo (and its aftermath) even though it is the personal lives of his characters which are at its center and not the historical events in which they are caught up, suggests that his imagination seized on some essential connection between his idea of (the Victorian) Vanity Fair and the Napoleonic conflicts.

At one point in the novel the connection becomes explicit, though it is muted in a parenthesis; it is when Pitt Crawley and Lady Southdown concert a strategy for approaching (the rich) Miss Crawley:

> "And if I might suggest, my sweet lady," Pitt said in a bland tone, "it would be as well not to take our precious Emily, who is too enthusiastic; but rather that you should be accompanied by our sweet and dear Lady Jane."
> "Most certainly, Emily would ruin everything," Lady Southdown said: and this time agreed to forgo her usual practice, which was, as we have said, before she bore down personally upon any individual whom she proposed to subjugate, to fire in a quantity of tracts upon the menaced party (as a charge of the French was always preceded by a furious cannonade). Lady Southdown, we say, for the sake of the invalid's health, or for the sake of her soul's ultimate welfare, or for the sake of her money, agreed to temporize.

The parenthesis, like a carefully laid mine, has an unexpected explosive effect. It is a means of comic, ironic deflation, and is so contrived as to hit two targets at once. On the one hand, Lady Southdown with her tracts, when compared to the French and their cannon, is made to appear a ridiculous (if determined) figure; on the other, the fierce French are conflated with an old woman, "tall and awful missionary of the truth" though she may be, and are reduced in turn. This kind of double deflationary effect is common to the host of military images that permeate the novel, for though it is only here that the novelist insinuates a direct analogy, the historical background is throughout so strongly rendered that any military image triggers an association with the Napoleonic wars. A special see-saw relation is thus established between activities at the Fair and the historic conflict: social battles, of whatever kind, are made absurd when compared to the real thing; historic battles, no matter how momentous, are implicitly reduced—amid a barrage of drawing-room war imagery—to an analagous scale. At the same time a major function of the Napoleonic setting becomes clear: the actual historic War becomes the ground for the metaphorical social war that is the novelist's subject. Life in Vanity Fair is more of a battle than a market. In this sense, as well as that advanced in the text, it may be said that "the French Emperor comes in to perform a part in this domestic comedy of Vanity Fair."

The war imagery is so pervasive that examples must be limited to a few representative instances. The imagery is mainly directed, following the emphasis in Bunyan, to evoking struggles for gain and attempts at sexual conquest in the Fair. "These money transactions—" we are told, apropos of the relations that pertain between Sir Pitt Crawley and his brother Bute, "these speculations in life and death—these silent battles for reversionary spoil—make brothers very loving towards each other in Vanity Fair." Both war and Fair images are combined in this passage; it is only the striking phrase "reversionary spoil" that animates it, however, and the last three words could in effect have been omitted. The struggle for such spoil lends itself to considerable elaboration:

> When Mrs. Bute took the command at Miss Crawley's house, the garrison there were charmed to act under such a leader, expecting all sorts of promotion from her promises, her generosity, and her kind words.

> That [Rawdon] would consider himself beaten, after one
> defeat, and make no attempt to regain the position he had
> lost, Mrs. Bute Crawley never allowed herself to suppose.
> She knew Rebecca to be too clever and spirited and des-
> perate a woman to submit without a struggle; and felt that
> she must prepare for that combat, and be incessantly
> watchful against assault, or mine, or surprise.
>   In the first place, though she held the town, was she sure
> of the principal inhabitant? Would Miss Crawley herself
> hold out . . . ?

Rawdon, who is ultimately deprived of his anticipated share of the
said spoil, is forced to fight his wars by other means and becomes
(among other skills that he develops) "a consummate master of bil-
liards":

> Like a great general, his genius used to rise with the dan-
> ger, and when the luck had been unfavourable to him for
> a whole game, and the bets were consequently against
> him, he would, with consummate skill and boldness, make
> some prodigious hits which would restore the battle, and
> come in a victor at the end, to the astonishment of every-
> body—of everybody, that is, who was a stranger to his
> play. Those who were accustomed to see it were cautious
> how they staked their money against a man of such sudden
> resources, and brilliant and overpowering skill.

Sexual conquests follow the same pattern; and though Glorvina
O'Dowd's intentions are no doubt more honorable than those of
Lord Steyne, they take much the same form: "[Lady O'Dowd and
Glorvina] agreed between themselves on this point, that Glorvina
should marry Major Dobbin, and were determined that the Major
should have no rest until the arrangement was brought about.
Undismayed by forty or fifty previous defeats, Glorvina laid siege to
him." In his pursuit of Becky, Lord Steyne decides she should be
relieved of all unnecessary encumbrances, and so first disposes of her
son and then of her companion: "it was clear that honest Briggs must
not lose her chance of settlement for life; and so she and her bags
were packed, and she set off on her journey. And so two of Rawdon's
out-sentinels were in the hands of the enemy."
    The war imagery is seen most clearly as a controlling principle

in the depiction of the lives of Becky and Amelia. The title of chapter
2 is "In which Miss Sharp and Miss Sedley prepare to open the
Campaign"; and though the particular campaign that the two young
ladies are intent not only on opening but on bringing to a speedy
conclusion is the capturing of a husband, the image—since the previous chapter details their departure from Miss Pinkerton's academy—refers as well to their embarking on the larger and more general
battle of life. The way Becky and Amelia wage the more general war
is in keeping with their characters, and follows the lines of two main
alternatives open to combatants in such a struggle—to conquer or
surrender. From the early stage in the narrative, therefore, the war
imagery gives rise to two implicit but controlling metaphors that
define the contrasted roles of the protagonists.

Thackeray himself seems, somewhat tentatively, to have thought
of Becky as a Napoleon. Edgar F. Harden says that she is "in fact, a
kind of female Napoleon, a clever leader who excites great interest
and certain kinds of frantic devotion in the men around her. . . . The
identification reaches its climax in Chapter LXIV. . . , where an
original woodcut portrays Becky in exile, dressed like Napoleon,
with spy-glass in hand." Since Thackeray did his own illustrations to
the text, that woodcut has considerable force. In the text itself, however, the novelist is more reserved: on one occasion Becky's admiring husband tells her she is "fit to be Commander-in-Chief, or
Archbishop of Canterbury, by Jove"; and on another is said to believe in her "as much as the French soldiers in Napoleon." Though
Becky's career may be viewed as that of an upstart who rises to great
heights before she meets her Waterloo, it seems to me that, on the
mercenary and predatory field of the Fair, we are led to think of her,
more appropriately, as a soldier of fortune. What we witness, as she
sets out on that aforementioned campaign, is her attempt to forage
where she can and by whatever means as she attempts to take society
by storm. Amelia, by contrast, is a much more passive figure. She
may be seen, again implicitly, as an unwilling conscript in the battles
that engulf her, defeatist by temperament, wanting always to opt out
of the fight, and ready to give in. In the opening description of her
it is clearly suggested how easily she collapses, all fight knocked out
of her: "even" Miss Pinkerton, we are told, "[ceases] scolding her
after the first time," and gives orders to everyone "to treat Miss
Sedley with the utmost gentleness, as harsh treatment [is] injurious
to her."

Becky's campaign, with its attendant strategies, is her pilgrim's progress in the world of Vanity Fair; but, since the campaign is her whole life, I shall refer only to some of the main stages in her progress, indicating how these are informed by the military imagery. Becky starts with neither status nor possessions, being a penniless orphan, the daughter of an artist and an opera girl. All she has are the natural resources with which she is endowed, her quick wits and her "famous frontal development" (among other physical attractions). The first stage in the campaign consists in the securing of a firm base from which to conduct operations, and to that end Becky sets out to get a husband. Jos ("this big beau") is the first man who presents himself and she determines "in her heart upon making the conquest" of him. When he escapes her, she turns her attentions to Rawdon Crawley; and the "skirmishes" which "[pass] perpetually [between them] during the little campaign" are always "similar in result": "The Crawley heavy cavalry [is] maddened by defeat, and routed every day" until Becky becomes Mrs. Rawdon. Nor is Rawdon the only one who is put to rout. In the face of enemies, Becky is even more devastating, as she shows in the case of George Osborne, whom she intuitively knows has come between Jos and herself. When she meets George at Miss Crawley's and he tries to patronize her, Becky exhibits the "presence of mind" which always characterizes her in the field (though she does lose it on one occasion when Sir Pitt proposes to her); she at once goes over to the attack and is so "cool and killing" as to cause "the Lieutenant's entire discomfiture." Showing too that she knows how to follow up an advantage, Becky presses home the attack until George is "utterly routed."

Becky makes her debut at the famous ball that "a noble Duchess" gives at Brussels on the eve of the Battle of Waterloo. She arrives late: "Her face was radiant; her dress perfection. In the midst of the great persons assembled, and the eye-glasses directed to her, Rebecca seemed to be as cool and collected as when she used to marshall Miss Pinkerton's little girls to church." The effect is subtle. To be "cool and collected" is presented as a distinctly soldierly quality: when Rawdon leaves for the battle next morning, it is said that "no man in the British army which has marched away, not the great Duke himself, could be more cool or collected in the presence of doubts and difficulties, than the indomitable little aide-de-camp's wife." As the eye-glasses are directed to Becky, therefore, it is neatly suggested how she comes under fire. And the reference to the peaceful little girls going to church sustains the implied image, for Becky's task then was to "marshall" the girls. There is no doubt, at all events, about the view we are intended to take of what she does next. Making her way through "fifty would-be partners," Becky heads straight for where Amelia is sitting "quite unnoticed, and dismally unhappy"; and in order "to finish" her forthwith, proceeds "to patronize her," remaining with her until she claims her husband George as a partner: "Women only know how to wound so. There is a poison on the tips of their little shafts, which stings a thousand times more than a man's blunter weapon. Our poor Emmy, who had never hated, never sneered all her life, was powerless in the hands of her remorseless little enemy."

Moving from one victory to another, Becky goes from Brighton to Brussels and then to Paris "during [the] famous winter" after Waterloo: "Lady Bareacres and the chiefs of the English society, stupid and irreproachable females, writhed in anguish at the success of the little upstart Becky, whose poisoned jokes quivered and rankled in their chaste breasts. But she had all the men on her side. She fought the women with indomitable courage, and they could not talk scandal in any tongue but their own." In London, however, though she quickly becomes "the vogue . . . among a certain class," the ladies shut their doors on her; and it is she who has to restrain her enraged husband: "You can't shoot me into society," she says to him "good-naturedly." Instead she uses her talents to engineer a presentation at Court, and then to secure an invitation to Gaunt House. At Gaunt House the ladies are frigid, but Becky proceeds to attack Lady Bareacres with such spirit and malice that she is forced to "[retreat] to a table, where she [begins] to look at pictures with great energy." By the end of the evening, with the men "crowded round the piano" at which she is singing, and "the women, her enemies, . . . left quite alone," Becky has another "great triumph." Thereafter Lady Steyne "succumbs" before Becky, and "the younger ladies of the House of Gaunt" are "also compelled into submission," though they occasionally still "set people at her":

> Mr. Wagg, the celebrated wit, and a led captain and trencherman of my Lord Steyne, was caused by the ladies to charge her; and the worthy fellow, leering at his patroness, and giving them a wink, as much as to say, "Now look out for sport," one evening began an assault upon Becky,

who was unsuspiciously eating her dinner. The little woman attacked on a sudden, but never without arms, lighted up in an instant, parried and riposted with a home-thrust, which made Wagg's face tingle with shame; then she returned to her soup with the most perfect calm and a quiet smile on her face.

If Becky is thus pictured as a intrepid fighter, it should be stressed that she is also repeatedly shown to use her weapons with the greatest ruthlessness and unscrupulousness. This characterizes her exploitation of all the men round her, including her husband and Lord Steyne. It is in relation to Steyne's pursuit of her that the novelist gives a fine turn to the line of military imagery. Steyne proceeds to lay siege to her, disposing methodically, as we have seen, of Rawdon's "out-sentinels," and then of the chief guard himself. Since the fortress does not in fact fall to Steyne's attack, however—for Rawdon returns home in time, it seems, to prevent actual sexual misdemeanor and the question of Becky's guilt (as we have also seen) is left open—her defeat does not take place in the field, so to speak. But she loses everything she has so carefully amassed—husband, possessions, the bubble reputation she has meticulously guarded—and is said to have "come to this bankruptcy," an exhaustion of resources that even a campaigner as resourceful as she may be reduced to. She soldiers on, however, as best she can, and finally restores her fortunes, we are told, after she encounters Jos again and makes short shrift of him—the victim at whom she first directed her fire.

The war imagery is less direct in the case of Amelia, the unwilling conscript who avoids battle whenever she can, but it shapes her presentation too. The schoolgirl, who is said (in the opening description of her) to "cry over a dead canary-bird; or over a mouse, that the cat has haply seized upon" (not to mention over "the end of a novel, were it ever so stupid"), is destined—when she is eventually dragged onto the battlefield—to be overwhelmed by the slaughter. The role that she then adopts is to bemoan the dead. She is drawn, willy-nilly, into the social war when her father is ruined and Mr. Osborne in "a brutal letter" announces the severing of relations between his family and hers. Her response is to "[pine] silently," and to "[die] away day by day." When her father, in return, demands that she "banish George from her mind, and . . . return all the presents and letters" she has had from him, she is unable to part with the letters and places them "back in her bosom again—as you have seen a woman nurse a child that is dead." Where Becky collects trophies as she goes, Amelia is left to contemplate the relics of a past conquest: "It was over these few worthless papers that she brooded and brooded. She lived in her past life—every letter seemed to recall some circumstance of it. How well she remembered them all! His looks and tones, his dress, what he said and how—these relics and remembrances of dead affection were all that were left her in the world. And the business of her life, was—to watch the corpse of Love."

Amelia's making it the business of her life to watch the corpse of Love is one of the most powerful images in the novel. Since George's love for her seems, at this point, to have been killed by his father's prohibition (and in fact is only resuscitated by Dobbin's interventions and George's own instinctive resistance to his father), it is a love which has itself gone dead, and Amelia's making it the "business" of her life to mourn its demise suggests the emotional bankruptcy of her own position in the Fair, a bankruptcy as far-reaching as her father's financial crash. The metaphor of "the corpse of Love," moreover, has an astonishing proleptic force, and leads straight to an actual battlefield. When George (married to Amelia, in the end, but having speedily proposed an elopement to Becky) is killed, "lying on his face, dead, with a bullet through his heart" at Waterloo, what Amelia precisely proceeds to do is to make it the bankrupt business of her life to watch his corpse. She hangs "her husband's miniature" over her bed, "the same little bed from which the poor girl [went] to his; and to which she [retires] now for many long, silent, tearful, but happy years." She may be said to pass happy years in corpse-watching, but they are years in which she defrauds both Dobbin and herself of life. Indeed, her retirement to that little bed is not only a withdrawal into a self-imposed and self-restored virginity, though she has borne a son; it is also a strategic retreat from the perils and challenges of life's battles.

For years Amelia devotes herself to the raising of her son. Where Becky, the dashing soldier of fortune, lives off the pickings of the field, lives, that is, off anyone and everyone available; Amelia, the victim of a literal war, "made by nature for a victim," nursing her long wound in private, "[lives] upon" her son, who is "her being." Though she retreats from the field of battle, she takes her place in the field of the Fair, where everyone tries to live on or off everyone else. Her subtle emotional parasitism, as she lives on her son's substance, is no better than Becky's blatant financial variety as she consumes the property of a Raggles—and perhaps no less ruinous in effect, though Georgy is not shown to grow up into a son and a lover. Amelia, however, is forced into one last unwilling battle over Georgy. Since it is "her nature . . . to yield," the ultimate outcome is not unexpected, but when she is cornered, she does make an initial stand and fight. Georgy's grandfather makes a formal offer to take him "and make him heir to the fortune which he . . . intended that his father should inherit," promises her a decent allowance, but stipulates that the child must "live entirely with his grandfather." Amelia at first rejects the offer, but then is led by her mother to feel that in "her selfishness" she is "sacrificing the boy." She nevertheless tries to fight back by seeking to give lessons and so add to the income of her father's struggling household, but that comes to nothing: "Poor simple lady, tender and weak—how are you to battle with the struggling violent world?" The "combat" lasts for weeks in her heart, but she gives way daily "before the enemy with whom she [has] to battle": "One truth after another was marshalling itself silently against her, keeping its ground. Poverty and misery for all, want and degradation for her parents, injustice to the boy—one by one the outworks of the little citadel were taken, in which the poor soul passionately guarded her only love and treasure." And in the end she admits defeat: "She was conquered, and laying down her arms, as it were, she humbly submitted. That day [Miss Osborne and she] arranged together the preliminaries of the treaty of capitulation." The capitulation firmly locates the battle in the Fair, for it is to its mercenary values that Amelia capitulates here, accepting that financial advantage means more to a boy than a mother's love. This capitulation precedes her ultimate surrender to Dobbin, who has lain in weary wait for her for years—and is rewarded with a boon (if not a booty) that he hardly wants by then.

If the narrative method subtly compensates for the absence of a plot and holds the narrative together from without, the war imagery effectively unifies it from within. It binds together the manifold activities that are depicted in the narrative, for where these are not directly rendered in its terms, they implicitly fall within its encompassing frame of reference. It also firmly links the personal and historical conflicts which are the distinct and apparently disjunctive components of the narrative; and, furthermore, joins the stories of Becky and Amelia, the two protagonists, and holds them together in constantly contrasted balance even when they seem to strain apart in centrifugal disarray. *Vanity Fair,* despite its inconsistent narrator and seemingly divided world, is all of a piece.

Chronology

1811	William Makepeace Thackeray born on July 18 to Richmond Thackeray, a British Civil Servant, and Anne Becher Thackeray, in the British colony of Calcutta.
1815	Richmond Thackeray dies of a fever.
1817	William is sent to school in England.
1822–28	Attends the Charterhouse School in London, where he circulates drawings and writes a poem called "Cabbages," a parody of a popular sentimental poem of the time.
1829	Enters Trinity College, Cambridge, where he contributes to the magazines *The Snob* and *The Gownsman,* his first publication being a poem, "Timbuctoo," in mockery of the year's Prize Poem competition (which is eventually won by Alfred Tennyson). In the summer, Thackeray makes his first trip to Paris.
1830	In June, after losing £1500 by gambling, Thackeray leaves Cambridge without earning his degree. In July he travels to Germany, where he spends a year. Meets Goethe in Weimar.
1831–32	Returns to London, where he enters the Middle Temple to study law. Passes the summer of 1832 in Paris.
1833	From May to August Thackeray writes and studies art in Paris. Loses the bulk of his inheritance because of a bank failure in India.
1835	Meets Isabella Shaw.
1836	Thackeray's first book, *Flore et Zephyr,* a set of comic lithographs of ballet dancers, is published. In August, Thackeray marries Isabella Shaw in Paris. Writes as Paris

correspondent for *The Constitutional* and contributes to several other magazines.

1837–38   The Thackerays settle in London. *The Yellowplush Correspondence* appears in *Fraser's Magazine.*

1839–40   *Catherine; a Story* appears in *Fraser's.*

1840   Thackeray's first book published in England, *The Paris Sketch Book.* Thackeray continues to contribute comic pieces and art criticism to several journals. Harriet Marian (Minny) Thackeray is born; Isabella Thackeray suffers a nervous breakdown which leads eventually to permanent insanity.

1841   *Comic Tales and Sketches,* edited and illustrated by Mr. Michael Angelo Titmarsh, appears in two volumes.

1842   Thackeray contributes "The Legend of Jawbrahim-Heraudee" to *Punch,* his first known work for the magazine.

1843   *The Irish Sketch Book,* by M. A. Titmarsh; this is Thackeray's first book to contain his own name, in the dedication.

1844   *Barry Lyndon* appears in *Fraser's Magazine* from January to December, with an interruption in October; because of limited popularity, Thackeray does not find a publisher for it. Thackeray works variously as a reviewer, political correspondent, and translator.

1845   Several publishers reject the first chapters of *Vanity Fair.*

1846   *The Book of Snobs* in *Punch.* Thackeray produces his first Christmas book, *Mrs. Perkin's Ball,* by M. A. Titmarsh.

1847–48   Bradbury and Evans, the publishers of *Punch,* release *Vanity Fair. Pen and Pencil Sketches of English Society* in twenty parts, from January 1847 through July 1848 (final double number). The novel appears in book form as *Vanity Fair. A Novel without a Hero.* Thackeray begins *Pendennis.*

1850   *Pendennis* concluded.

1851   Thackeray lectures on the eighteenth-century English humorists. Begins *Henry Esmond.* Resigns from *Punch* in December.

1852   *Henry Esmond* is published in three volumes by Smith, Elder. Thackeray visits America for the first time.

1853   Thackeray returns to England. Begins *The Newcomes.*

The first of twenty-four parts appears in October, published by Bradbury and Evans.

1854 Thackeray produces *The Rose and the Ring,* the last of his Christmas books, and writes a comedy entitled *The Wolves and the Lamb* (later novelized as *Lovel the Widower*).

1855 *Miscellanies: Prose and Verse* is published by Bradbury and Evans. Thackeray concludes *The Newcomes.* Makes second trip to America. Lectures on the four Georges.

1857 Thackeray runs for Parliament from Oxford, unsuccessfully. The first number of *The Virginians* appears.

1859 *The Virginians* concluded.

1860 The first issue of *The Cornhill Magazine,* edited by Thackeray, appears. Thackeray's contributions include *Lovel the Widower* (in six numbers) and *The Four Georges.*

1861 *The Adventures of Philip* appears in *Cornhill.*

1862 Resigns editorship of *Cornhill,* concludes *The Adventures of Philip.* Begins writing *Denis Duval.*

1863 *Denis Duval* (uncompleted) appears in *Cornhill.* On the morning of December 24, Thackeray dies at the age of fifty-two.

Contributors

HAROLD BLOOM, Sterling Professor of the Humanities at Yale University, is the author of *The Anxiety of Influence, Poetry and Repression,* and many other volumes of literary criticism. His forthcoming study, *Freud: Transference and Authority,* attempts a full-scale reading of all of Freud's major writings. A MacArthur Prize Fellow, he is general editor of five series of literary criticism published by Chelsea House. During 1987–88, he was appointed Charles Eliot Norton Professor of Poetry at Harvard University.

DOROTHY VAN GHENT taught at Kansas University and the University of Vermont. Her numerous publications include *The English Novel: Form and Function* and *Keats: The Myth of the Hero.*

BARBARA HARDY is Professor of English Literature at Birkbeck College, University of London. Her books include critical studies of George Eliot, Jane Austen, Charles Dickens, and William Makepeace Thackeray.

WOLFGANG ISER teaches English and Comparative Literature at the University of Konstanz in Germany and the University of California, Irvine. A pioneer of "reception aesthetics" criticism and a founder of the "Poetics and Hermeneutics" research group, he is the author of *The Act of Reading, The Implied Reader,* and *Der Appelstruktur der Texte,* among other books.

ROBERT E. LOUGY is Professor of English at Pennsylvania State University. His publications include studies of Dickens, Thackeray, Swinburne, and nineteenth-century poetics. The author of *Charles Robert Maturin,* he has recently edited *The Children and the Chapel.*

MARIA DIBATTISTA is Associate Professor of English at Princeton University. She is the author of *Virginia Woolf's Major Novels: The Fable of Anon*.

ROBERT M. POLHEMUS is Professor of English at Stanford University. He is the author of *The Changing World of Anthony Trollope* and *Comic Faith: The Great Tradition from Austen to Joyce*.

H. M. DALESKI, Professor of English Literature at the Hebrew University of Jerusalem, is the author of *The Forked Flame: A Study of D. H. Lawrence*, *Dickens and the Art of Analogy*, and *Joseph Conrad: The Way of Dispossession*.

Bibliography

Burch, Mark H. " 'The World Is a Looking Glass': *Vanity Fair* as Satire." *Genre* 15, no. 3 (1982): 265–79.

Carey, John. *Thackeray: Prodigal Genius*. London: Faber and Faber, 1977.

Chapman, Raymond. *The Victorian Debate: English Literature and Society 1832–1901*. New York: Basic Books, 1968.

Colby, Robert A. *Thackeray's Canvass of Humanity: An Author and His Public*. Columbus: Ohio State University Press, 1979.

Dooley, D. J. "Thackeray's Use of Vanity Fair." *Studies in English Literature 1500–1900* 11, no. 4 (1971): 701–13.

Ennis, Lambert. *Thackeray: The Sentimental Cynic*. Evanston: Northwestern University Press, 1950.

Ferris, Ina. *William Makepeace Thackeray*. Boston: Twayne, 1983.

Frazer, John P. "George IV and Jos Sedley in *Vanity Fair*." *English Language Notes* 19, no. 2 (1981): 122–28.

Hagan, John. *"Vanity Fair:* Becky Brought to Book Again." *Studies in the Novel* 7 (1975): 479–505.

Harden, Edgar F. *The Emergence of Thackeray's Serial Fiction*. Athens: The University of Georgia Press, 1979.

Hardy, Barbara. *The Exposure of Luxury: Radical Themes in Thackeray*. London: Peter Owen, 1972.

Klein, J. T. "The Dual Center: A Study of Narrative Structure in *Vanity Fair*." *College Literature* 4, no. 2 (1977): 122–28.

Lerner, Lawrence. "Thackeray and Marriage." *Essays in Criticism* 25, no. 3 (1975): 279–303.

Lester, John A., Jr. "Thackeray's Narrative Technique." *PMLA* 69 (1954): 392–409.

Loofbourow, John. *Thackeray and the Form of Fiction*. Princeton: Princeton University Press, 1964.

Martin, Bruce K. *"Vanity Fair:* Narrative Ambivalence and Comic Form." *Tennessee Studies in Literature* 20 (1975): 37–49.

McMaster, Juliet. *Thackeray: The Major Novels*. Toronto: University of Toronto Press, 1971.

Miller, J. Hillis. *The Form of Victorian Fiction: Thackeray, Dickens, Trollope, George Eliot, Meredith and Hardy*. Notre Dame: University of Notre Dame Press, 1968.

Milner, Ian. "Theme and Moral Vision in Thackeray's *Vanity Fair.*" *Philologica Pragensia* 13, no. 4 (1970): 177–85.

Musselwhite, David. "Notes on a Journey to Vanity Fair." *Literature and History: A Journal for the Humanities* 7, no. 1 (1981): 62–90.

Paris, Bernard J. *A Psychological Approach to Fiction: Studies in Thackeray, Stendhal, George Eliot, Dostoevsky, and Conrad.* Bloomington: Indiana University Press, 1974.

Phillips, Kenneth C. *The Language of Thackeray.* London: Andre Deutsch, 1978.

Ray, Gordon N. "*Vanity Fair:* One Version of the Novelist's Responsibility." *Essays by Divers Hands: Being the Transactions of the Royal Society of Literature in the United Kingdom* n.s. 25 (1950): 87–101.

Redwine, Bruce. "The Uses of Memento Mori in *Vanity Fair.*" *Studies in English Literature* 17, no. 4 (1977): 657–72.

Shillingsburg, Peter L., ed. *Costerus* n.s 2 (1974). Special Thackeray edition.

Stevenson, Richard C. "The Problem of Judging Becky Sharp: Scene and Narrative Commentary in *Vanity Fair.*" *Victorian Institute Journal* 6 (1977): 1–8.

Sundell, M. G., ed. *Twentieth Century Interpretations of* Vanity Fair. Englewood Cliffs, N.J.: Prentice-Hall, 1969.

Sutherland, John A. "The Expanding Narrative of *Vanity Fair.*" *Journal of Narrative Technique* 3, no. 3 (1973): 149–69.

———. *Thackeray at Work.* London: Athlone, 1974.

Tillotson, Geoffrey. *Thackeray the Novelist.* Cambridge: Cambridge University Press, 1954.

——— and Donald Hawes, eds. *Thackeray: The Critical Heritage.* London: Routledge & Kegan Paul, 1968.

———. *A View of Victorian Literature.* Oxford: Clarendon, 1974.

Welsh, Alexander, ed. *Thackeray: A Collection of Critical Essays.* Englewood Cliffs, N.J.: Prentice-Hall, 1968.

Wheatley, James F. *Patterns in Thackeray's Fiction.* Cambridge, Mass.: M.I.T. University Press, 1969.

Williams, Ioan. *The Realist Novel in England: A Study in Development.* London: Macmillan, 1974.

Wolff, Cynthia Griffin. "Who Is the Narrator of *Vanity Fair* and Where Is He Standing?" *College Literature* 1, no. 3 (1974): 190–203.

Vega-Ritter, Max. "Women under Judgement in *Vanity Fair.*" *Cahiers d'Etudes et de Recherches Victoriennes et Edouardiennes* 3 (1976): 7–24.

Acknowledgments

"On *Vanity Fair*" by Dorothy Van Ghent from *The English Novel: Form and Function* by Dorothy Van Ghent, © 1953 by Dorothy Van Ghent. Reprinted by permission of the Estate of Dorothy Van Ghent and Harper & Row Publishers.

"Art and Nature" by Barbara Hardy from *The Exposure of Luxury: Radical Themes in Thackeray* by Barbara Hardy, © 1972 by Barbara Hardy. Reprinted by permission of the author and the publisher, Peter Owen Ltd., London.

"The Reader in the Realistic Novel: Esthetic Effects in Thackeray's *Vanity Fair*" (originally entitled "The Reader as a Component Part of the Realistic Novel: Esthetic Effects in Thackeray's *Vanity Fair*") by Wolfgang Iser from *The Implied Reader: Patterns of Communication in Prose Fiction from Bunyan to Beckett* by Wolfgang Iser, © 1974 by the Johns Hopkins University Press, Baltimore/ London. Reprinted by permission of the Johns Hopkins University Press.

"Vision and Satire: The Warped Looking Glass in *Vanity Fair*" by Robert E. Lougy from *PMLA* 90, no. 2 (March 1975), © 1975 by the Modern Language Association of America. Reprinted by permission of the Modern Language Association of America.

"The Triumph of Clytemnestra: The Charades in *Vanity Fair*" by Maria DiBattista from *PMLA* 95, no. 5 (October 1980), © 1980 by the Modern Language Association of America. Reprinted by permission of the Modern Language Association of America.

"The Comedy of Shifting Perspectives" (originally entitled "Thackeray's *Vanity Fair* (1847–48): The Comedy of Shifting Perspectives") by Robert M. Polhemus from *Comic Faith: The Great Tradition from Austen to Joyce* by Robert M. Polhemus, © 1980 by the University of Chicago. Reprinted by permission of the University of Chicago Press.

"Strategies in *Vanity Fair*" by H. M. Daleski from *Unities: Studies in the English Novel* by H. M. Daleski, © 1985 by the University of Georgia Press. Reprinted by permission of the University of Georgia Press.

Index